A Matter of Trust: Connecting Teachers and
Learners in the Early Childhood Classroom
CAROLLEE HOWES & SHARON RITCHIE

The Power of Projects:
Meeting Contemporary Challenges in Early
Childhood Classrooms—Strategies and Solutions
JUDY HARRIS HELM & SALLEE BENEKE, Eds.

Bringing Learning to Life: The Reggio Approach
to Early Childhood Education
LOUISE BOYD CADWELL

Widening the Circle: Including Children with
Disabilities in Preschool Programs
SAMUEL L. ODOM, Ed.

Children with Special Needs:
Lessons for Early Childhood Professionals
MARJORIE J. KOSTELNIK, ESTHER ETSUKO ONAGA,
BARBARA ROHDE, & ALICE PHIPPS WHIREN

Developing Constructivist Early Childhood
Curriculum: Practical Principles and Activities
RHETA DeVRIES, BETTY ZAN,
CAROLYN HILDEBRANDT, REBECCA EDMIASTON,
& CHRISTINA SALES

Outdoor Play:
Teaching Strategies with Young Children
JANE PERRY

Embracing Identities in Early Childhood
Education: Diversity and Possibilities
SUSAN GRIESHABER & GAILE S. CANNELLA, Eds.

Bambini:
The Italian Approach to Infant/Toddler Care
LELLA GANDINI & CAROLYN POPE EDWARDS, Eds.

Educating and Caring for Very Young Children:
The Infant/Toddler Curriculum
DORIS BERGEN, REBECCA REID, & LOUIS TORELLI

Young Investigators:
The Project Approach in the Early Years
JUDY HARRIS HELM & LILIAN G. KATZ

Serious Players in the Primary Classroom:
Empowering Children Through Active Learning
Experiences, 2nd Edition
SELMA WASSERMANN

Telling a Different Story:
Teaching and Literacy in an Urban Preschool
CATHERINE WILSON

Young Children Reinvent Arithmetic:
Implications of Piaget's Theory, 2nd Edition
CONSTANCE KAMII

Supervision in Early Childhood Education:
A Developmental Perspective, 2nd Edition
JOSEPH J. CARUSO & M. TEMPLE FAWCETT

The Early Childhood Curriculum:
A Review of Current Research, 3rd Edition
CAROL SEEFELDT, Ed.

Leadership in Early Childhood:
The Pathway to Professionalism, 2nd Edition
JILLIAN RODD

Inside a Head Start Center:
Developing Policies from Practice
DEBORAH CEGLOWSKI

Uncommon Caring:
Learning from Men Who Teach Young Children
JAMES R. KING

Teaching and Learning in a Diverse World:
Multicultural Education for Young Children,
2nd Edition
PATRICIA G. RAMSEY

Windows on Learning:
Documenting Young Children's Work
JUDY HARRIS HELM, SALLEE BENEKE,
& KATHY STEINHEIMER

Bringing Reggio Emilia Home: An Innovative
Approach to Early Childhood Education
LOUISE BOYD CADWELL

Major Trends and Issues in Early Childhood
Education: Challenges, Controversies, and Insights
JOAN P. ISENBERG & MARY RENCK JALONGO, Eds.

Master Players: Learning from Children at Play
GRETCHEN REYNOLDS & ELIZABETH JONES

Understanding Young Children's Behavior:
A Guide for Early Childhood Professionals
JILLIAN RODD

Understanding Quantitative and Qualitative
Research in Early Childhood Education
WILLIAM L. GOODWIN & LAURA D. GOODWIN

Diversity in the Classroom: New Approaches to
the Education of Young Children, 2nd Edition
FRANCES E. KENDALL

(Continued)

A Matter of Trust

CONNECTING TEACHERS AND LEARNERS IN THE EARLY CHILDHOOD CLASSROOM

Carollee Howes
Sharon Ritchie

FOREWORD BY BARBARA T. BOWMAN

TEACHERS COLLEGE PRESS

Teachers College, Columbia University
New York and London

Published by Teachers College Press, 1234 Amsterdam Avenue, New York, NY 10027

Library of Congress Cataloging-in-Publication Data

Howes, Carollee.
    A matter of trust : connecting teachers and learners in the early childhood classroom / Carollee Howes, Sharon Ritchie ; foreword by Barbara T. Bowman.
      p. cm.—(Early childhood education series)
    Includes bibliographical references and index.
    ISBN 0-8077-4265-1 (alk. paper)—ISBN 0-8077-4264-3 (pbk. : alk. paper)
    1. Early childhood education. 2. Teacher-student relationships. I. Ritchie, Sharon.
    II. Title. III. Early childhood education series (Teachers College Press)

LB1139.23 .H69 2002
372.21—dc21   2002021759

ISBN 0-8077-4264-3 (paper)
ISBN 0-8077-4265-1 (cloth)

Printed on acid-free paper

Manufactured in the United States of America

09 08 07 06 05 04 03 02   8 7 6 5 4 3 2 1

Contents

Foreword

In the United States over the past century, we have substantially altered our views about how best to care for and educate young children. Social and economic changes have often driven our conception of children's needs and the social policies and educational practices necessary to secure their well-being. The science of child development has played an increasingly important role in helping to define these.

Recent changes in social and economic conditions in the United States have again challenged how we care for and educate young children. Two trends are especially relevant. One is the need for increased workforce preparation. Higher standards of education are foreseen as critical to the transition from an industrial to a technological society. Child development research has shown that early learning lays the basis for school success and that early intervention for children at risk can change children's educational trajectory, bringing early education to the forefront of public attention.

The second change is the increasing number of mothers in the workforce, particularly low-income mothers. Many families cannot be solely responsible for the care of their young children. Given the relationship between early experience and later development, the quality of out-of-home programs for children between birth and school age has gained in importance.

Responding to these new challenges has not been easy. The tension among child-rearing goals for basic care, social/emotional development, and preparation for school has often divided the professional community and confused parents planning for their children and governments leaders developing policies for early childhood programs. One of the salutary developments of the last few years is the coming together of the research and practice literature around the interrelationship of care, social and intellectual development, and school learning (Bredekamp & Copple, 1997) and the importance of mother/teacher/caregiver to children's development and learning.

The early research identified structural dimensions of schools and centers—group size, ratio, teacher training—as proxies for the program quality (Howes, Phillips, & Whitebook, 1992). However, the field clearly needed to define in much better detail the nature of the interactions between children and their teachers/caregivers that accounted for positive learning outcomes.

For the last few years there has been an increasing interest in children's relationships as predictors of their educational competence. A number of researchers, among them Carollee Howes, have used the emotional component of the caregiver/child relationship as the critical variable. These studies are built on a theoretical model for teacher/caregiver relationships with children similar to that found in mother/child relationship and suggest that the quality of these relationships can be reliably and validly assessed (Birch & Ladd, 1997; Bowlby, 1969; Howes & Smith, 1995; Pianta, 1999). This research points out that children's relationships with caregivers and teachers are emotionally significant and affect how children develop and what they learn (Bowman, Donovan, & Burns, 2001).

In their book, Carolee Howes and Sharon Ritchie have done the early childhood field an immense service by presenting their significant research on child-teacher relationships. In three major studies they conducted extensive observations in classrooms where teachers are working with children from difficult life circumstances. Through the use of narratives from these classrooms, Howes and Ritchie show how teachers can develop positive relationships with children whose previous child-adult relationships have been very troubled. Although building trusting relationships requires dedication and skill on the part of the teacher, the potential for children's learning in a harmonious classroom climate is greatly enhanced. With their book Carollee Howes and Sharon Ritchie provide a nuanced and useful guide for the early childhood community as we again use the science of child development to help us change our institutional arrangements to fit the needs of children.

—Barbara T. Bowman

REFERENCES

Birch, S. H., & Ladd, G. W. (1997). The child-teacher relationship and children's early school adjustment. *Journal of School Psychology, 35,* 61–79.

Bowlby, J. (1969). *Attachment and loss*, Vol. 1. New York: Basic Books.

Bowman, B., Donovan, M., Burns, S. (2001). *Eager to learn: Educating our preschoolers.* Washington, DC: National Academy Press.

Bredekamp, S., & Copple, C. (Eds.). (1997). *Developmentally appropriate practice in early childhood programs.* Washington, DC: National Association for the Education of Young Children.

Howes, C., Phillips, D., & Whitebook, M. (1992). Thresholds of quality: Implications for the social development of children in center-based child care. *Child Development, 63,* 449–460.

Howes, C., & Smith, E. (1995). Children and their child care teachers: Profiles of relationships. *Social Development, 4,* 44–61.

Pianta, R. C. (1999). *Enhancing relationships between children and teachers.* Washington, DC: American Psychological Association.

Acknowledgments

The teachers who participated in the Children with Difficult Life Circumstances Study and the Best Practices Project generously gave us permission to observe their work with children. Thank you for teaching us as well as the children. We would like to particularly thank the staff, children, and families at Saint John's Therapeutic Preschool in Santa Monica, CA. This program has emphasized the development of attachment relationships with young children for the past decade. The thoughtful work of the teachers provided us with many of our examples of positive work with children.

Many dedicated observers collected our narrative examples: Farnaz Benyamini, Jolena James, Rene McDonough, Maria Pak, Shira Rosenblatt, Holli Tonyan, and the UCLA Teacher Education class of 1998.

Karen Brodkin, Ellen Smith, and Billie Weiser read the manuscript in draft form and gave us important feedback. Thank you.

A Matter of Trust

Connecting Teachers and Learners in the Early Childhood Classroom

Introduction

In this book we focus on the development of positive child-teacher relationships in infant-toddler, preschool, and early elementary school classrooms. Drawing on our experiences as a developmental psychologist and a teacher educator, we examine the premise that teacher behaviors and classroom environments that enhance the development of positive child-teacher relationships are the same behaviors and arrangements that facilitate harmonious classrooms in which children can learn. We argue that positive child-teacher relationships are constructed in classrooms where both learning and social relationships are valued. We maintain that teacher attention to relationships—child-teacher relationships and child-child relationships—are associated with prosocial and cooperative classroom climates.

Increasingly, teachers of young children report that the children who enter their classrooms are difficult to manage and support. This teacher perception is supported by alarming statistics on the increase in numbers of children growing up in difficult life circumstances—maltreatment, parental psychopathology or substance abuse, and poverty. Too often these life circumstances and the resulting disorganization of caregiving systems within their families result in a profile of behaviors that teachers find challenging. Children bring with them to the classroom the behaviors and coping strategies they have developed in response to difficult and sometimes tragic experiences in their young lives. They can be hostile, and they often do not trust adults to care for them or to help them organize their worlds.

Our conversations with teachers suggest that they are searching for help in working successfully with children who are difficult. Teachers tell us that classroom management is at the root of their difficulties. They talk of being strict, of "not smiling until after the holiday break," of making children accountable. They ask for systems to instill discipline.

We agree that children facing difficult life circumstances often behave in challenging ways. Teachers and children too often engage in acrimonious behaviors that result in conflicts and the development of nontrusting relationships. Classroom climates become harsh and unwelcoming. Unfortunately, learning as well as social development suffers. When children are preoccupied with difficult child-teacher relationships, they are unable to benefit from the learning opportunities available in the classroom.

We begin this discussion with an example of how one child coping with difficult life circumstances disrupted classroom learning and how one teacher worked to change her patterns of relating and classroom behavior. Carolyn is a foster child, currently in her third out-of-home placement in her short 5 years. Her biological mother is in prison. Carolyn has only sporadic contact with her. In the narrative example that follows, Ms. Rosen, Carolyn's teacher, has gathered the children into a familiar classroom ritual—circle time. The learning goal is twofold. When it is their "turn," children are learning to produce a verbal narrative that others can understand; and when others have a "turn," children are learning to listen and comprehend the verbal narrations of another. In this context children cannot learn to produce and comprehend narratives if turn-taking is disrupted, if more than one person talks at a time, or if nonverbal behavior distracts the speakers or listeners.

> Carolyn stands up. Ms. Rosen says, "Carolyn, you can have a turn if you sit down, but you're not ready if you are standing up." Carolyn stays standing during the next child's turn, and then sits down.
>
> After a few more children have had their turn, Ms. Rosen says, "Carolyn, you are ready. Do you want to tell us what you did on your home days?" Carolyn says, "I'm mad at you." Ms. Rosen says, "But do you want to tell us what you did on your home days?" Carolyn says, "I played with my stove and with all my toys."
>
> Ms. Rosen engages with another child. Carolyn says to Ms. Rosen, "I'm mad at you." Ms. Rosen says, "That's okay," and continues her engagement with another child.
>
> The other children begin the transition to snack time, but Carolyn goes instead to the rocking chair and rocks facing backward. Ms. Rosen says, "So, Carolyn, come on and wash your hands."
>
> Carolyn continues to rock. "I want my mommy. I want my mommy. I want my mommy." Ms. Rosen is simultaneously helping children to get settled at the snack table and listening to Carolyn. Ms. Rosen reflects, "You want your mommy. You were home for two days. Is it hard to come back to school?" Carolyn says, "I don't want to come to school."

When Carolyn stands up in the middle of circle time she interrupts the child who is taking a turn. Her action draws the attention away from the speaker. Ms. Rosen, the teacher, knows that Carolyn's history of multiple out-of-home placements makes it difficult for the 5-year-old to create a trusting, positive relationship with Ms. Rosen. One goal of the teacher, then, is to construct a different and more trusting relationship with Carolyn than

Carolyn's prior adult-child relationship. However, as the teacher for the entire classroom of children, Ms. Rosen must simultaneously attend to Carolyn and preserve the learning context for all the classroom participants. Thus, she continues constructing her relationship with Carolyn by first coaching her through the turn-taking, narrative-producing classroom ritual, and then by focusing more directly on Carolyn's concerns. Rather than punishing Carolyn or removing her from the classroom, she helps her be part of the learning community. Ms. Rosen is convinced that as Carolyn moves toward a trusting child-teacher relationship, she will be a more successful participant in the school learning community. Our longitudinal observations of Carolyn are consistent with this belief (Howes & Ritchie, 1998).

Ms. Rosen is enacting an approach to children that we advocate in this book. It is based on the application of Bowlby's (1982) attachment theory to child-teacher relationships. We maintain that for children of all ages, the ability to learn depends on negotiating a trusting relationship with the teacher. Support for the approach we advocate comes from several sources. First, we used theory and empirical research based on mother-child attachment to examine processes involved in the construction of positive, collaborative, cooperative, and mutually reciprocal relationships. Such relationships mean that both partners are concerned about and responsive to the other and are invested in resolving conflict and establishing harmonious relationships. Within this theoretical framework, teachers do not *manage* children and classrooms; rather they work toward the construction and maintenance of responsible, reciprocated positive relationships.

A second source of support for our approach comes from a growing body of research on the independence of individual child-teacher attachment relationships from child-mother relationships. This research suggests that teachers and children can construct relationships different in quality from child-parent attachment relationships. The child-teacher relationships can be difficult when child-parent attachments are positive, and conversely, child-teacher relationships can be positive when child-parent relationships are problematic. That is, even if children have not been able to trust prior caregiving adults, current child-teacher relationships can be positive and compensate for difficult previous relationships.

Furthermore, the research on child-teacher relationships provides directions to identify teacher strategies for working successfully with children with difficult life circumstance. Although child-teacher relationship quality is independent of child-mother relationship quality, the ways in which child-teacher relationships are formed are very similar to the formation of child-mother relationships. Moreover, the quality of child-teacher attachment relationships has significant short- and long-term influences on children's development.

The third source of support for our approach—one that is demonstrated in the greatest detail in this book—is an ongoing program of developing case studies that document, through a combination of qualitative and quantitative research, practices in school settings that are successful in creating classroom climates that facilitate positive relationships.

Throughout this book we integrate materials from three different data sources: two longitudinal studies of children in preschool programs and a cross-sectional study of children in infant-toddler, preschool, and primary-grade classrooms. We use ethnographic material in the form of narratives that tell stories of interactions among children and their teachers and classmates in many classrooms. When appropriate, we review the quantitative data collected in many of these same classrooms. All of the children's and teacher's names have been changed to protect our agreements of confidentiality. Program names have been changed as well.

We assume that across children's development, positive child-teacher relationships will be facilitated by sensitive and responsive teacher involvement, clear and consistent classroom routines, and the creation of a mutually responsible community. We also assume that the particular strategies teachers use will change as children move from infancy to middle childhood. Therefore, we include narrative examples drawn from infant-toddler child care, preschool-age community child care, Head Start, and intervention programs and regular and after-school classrooms for kindergarten through third grade. We selected some of the school programs from which we draw narratives both because they served children with difficult life circumstances and because the teachers and program directors were reflective in their efforts to understand and construct positive child-teacher relationships. Other programs we describe also served children with difficult life circumstances, but approached children and learning in a more traditional manner.

DEVELOPING POSITIVE RELATIONSHIPS

Teachers and children begin to construct their relationships on the first day of school. Children enter classrooms with expectations of teacher behavior based on their relationship history with other teachers and their caregivers within their families. The following narrative occurred during the first week in a kindergarten classroom. As would have been the case for most teachers encountering a child for the first time, Ms. Lowett did not know about James's prior relationship history. In the course of the first hour of the morning on the first day of school, James is making himself known to his teacher. He is both resisting his teacher and attempting to control the classroom. As shown in the narratives that follow, Ms. Lowett is searching for a way to help him. She begins by excluding him from the classroom community but quickly changes her strategy, taking time to ask him to be a participant.

> Throughout circle time, James is calling out and talking back to Ms. Lowett. She repeatedly gives him warnings to quiet down and participate. James continues with the calling out and general disruption. Ms. Lowett takes him by the arm and removes him to the hall, outside the door. She tells him that he needs to sit there for at least 2 minutes and when he is ready to return he may.
>
> James rejoins the group on the rug. Almost immediately, he wiggles from his assigned seat until he is lying on his back. Ms. Lowett is introducing a song with a call–and–response format that includes calling out children's names. Ms. Lowett asks him if he wants his name called during the song. James says yes. Ms. Lowett tells him that he should sit up, so people will know that he wants to participate. He sits up and moves into the circle.
>
> Later that morning the children are at their desks. Ms. Lowett has written *STAR*, the acronym for a school rule, on a chart. The teacher guides the children in naming the letters, identifying what they stand for and what they mean. The class arrives at *A* and *act*, and Ms. Lowett asks James to tell her what he thinks *act* means. James tells her that act is "when you do something."

By changing her strategy so that she brings James into the learning community instead of excluding him in time out, the teacher tells James that he is part of the group; thus, he has responsibilities and gets a chance to demonstrate his knowledge.

Child-teacher relationships are not static. Teachers who intend to create positive relationships with children who are difficult report that the process is a long one. One teacher completing her first year of teaching third grade reflected that it took 6 months of daily one-on-one, after-class, relationship-building activities to move one particularly difficult child from anger, defiance, and refusal to do class work to grade-level performance and improved peer relations.

Because child-teacher relationships are an important first step in helping children explore and learn within the classroom environment, there is great value in teachers knowing *how* to help these children construct positive, trusting child-teacher relationships. Once children can trust the teacher, they can use her or him to organize and structure their learning (Birch & Ladd, 1997; Pianta, 1998; Howes & Smith, 1995b), as the teacher attends to their comments, is asked for help, and shares their discoveries.

The cognitive and social development that promotes learning in school occurs in an interactive context (Pianta & Walsh, 1996). Children who do not trust, but are instead preoccupied with the child-teacher relationship, are unable to use the teacher as a resource for learning and spend their time in school resisting, attempting to control, or avoiding the teacher. Their focus on the problematic relationship rather than on the content of school takes away from their ability to learn and may interfere with the learning of other children in the class.

THEORETICAL FRAMEWORK

As noted earlier, the theory that we use in framing our work is child-mother attachment theory (Bowlby, 1982). In the past decade, several theorists have expanded basic assumptions in Bowlby's attachment theory to encompass the notion of attachment networks as opposed to a theory that emphasizes the primacy of the child-mother attachment (Howes, 1999; Pianta, 1998; van IJzendoorn, Sagi, & Lambermon, 1992). In each of these formulations, teachers are considered attachment figures because they provide physical and emotional care and are consistent and predictable in children's lives. From the children's perspective these adults provide comfort and a secure base and serve to organize the children's behaviors in the classroom.

There is now a large body of evidence on the validity of assessing attachment relationships between children and teachers, identifying and examining antecedents of different qualities of relationships between children and their teachers, and examining the concurrent and long-term connections between the qualities of different relationships and children's social competence. We will review much of this material in subsequent chapters. In brief, the findings of these studies suggest that the quality of child-teacher attachment relationships can be reliably and validly assessed, that child-mother attachment relationships and child-alternative caregiver attachment relationships are similar in process, and that child-alternative-caregiver-attachment security predicts social competence in the short and long term (Howes, 1999). Children with more positive child-teacher relationships appear more able to make use of the learning opportunities available in classrooms (Howes & Smith, 1995b), construct more positive peer relationships (Howes, Matheson, & Hamilton, 1994), and better adjust to the demands of formal schooling (Birch & Ladd, 1997). The quality of children's early relationships with their teachers emerges as an important predictor of these children's future social relations with peers (Howes & Tonyan, 2000), their behavior problems (Howes & Aikins, in press), and school satisfaction and achievement (Baker, 1999; Peisner-Feinberg et al., 2001). If children feel emotionally secure with their teacher, they can use her or him as a secure base and a resource for exploring the learning opportunities of the classroom (Birch & Ladd, 1997; Howes, 2000).

More recent theoretical work on this topic has adopted a contextual perspective (Pianta, 1999). In particular, the social-emotional climate of the classroom, as well as the individual relationship between the child and teacher, is considered important in understanding the influences of child-teacher attachment relationships (Boyce et al., 1998). According to this perspective, individual child-teacher relationships and teacher perceptions of individual children's behavior problems are constructed within the context of classroom climates. The social-emotional climate of the classroom is defined by the level of aggression and other behavior problems in the group of children, the nature of child-teacher relationships, and the frequency and complexity of interaction with peers. Using this notion of classroom climate, we can describe classrooms on a continuum ranging from positive, prosocial environments characterized by close adult-child relationships, intricate peer play and cooperative work, and little disruptive behavior, to hostile environments characterized by conflictual child-teacher relationships, angry, disruptive children, and little constructive peer play or collaborative learning. Positive, prosocial classroom environments are communities in which all participants are responsible for learning.

Within this theoretical framework, classroom management can be reconceptualized as a process that creates positive child-teacher relationships. The construction of positive, prosocial classroom environments can be considered a substitute or supplement for traditional classroom management. If a teacher constructs positive, secure attachment relationships with children such that there is a predominance of what Kochanska (1997) calls mutually reciprocated relationships, then classroom management becomes an issue of constructing, maintaining, and sustaining harmonious interactions and relationships rather than a matter of finding strategies for managing and avoiding potential conflict.

MOVING FROM THEORY TO THE CLASSROOM

We undertook writing this book because we believe that as part of their preparation for teaching, teachers should be helped to recognize that all children need to trust teachers to care for them and to help them organize a scary world. At the same time, the needs and behaviors of children who are difficult may seem overwhelming to teachers. As we sought to help teachers work successfully with children growing up in difficult life circumstances, the following questions have provided direction:

- What kinds of behaviors do children with difficult life circumstances bring to classrooms, and how do these behaviors reflect their prior relationship history?

- How can teachers and children move from acrimonious to positive mutually reciprocal interactions?
- How can understanding children's prior experiences with child-adult relationships help teachers to construct new trusting child-adult relationships?
- What kinds of teacher behaviors and classroom organizations are associated with positive child-teacher relationships and prosocial classroom environments for children with difficult life circumstances?
- How do teachers balance the needs of individual children and still construct a mutually responsive and responsible community in which all children are learning?

In answering these questions throughout our text, we have organized our chapters into three parts. In Part I we describe different kinds of child-teacher relationships, explore how child-teacher relationships develop and change with attention to conflict and emotions, and describe how child-teacher relationships are related to classroom learning.

Part II focuses on teacher behaviors used in constructing positive and negative child-teacher relationships and classroom climates. We work from the theoretical assumption that the social behaviors of children and teachers are equally important in the construction of relationships, but that the responsibility for effective intervention rests with teachers working to construct different types of relationships with children.

Part III moves beyond the individual child-teacher relationships to include the construct of community. We define community as being achieved when teachers and children recognize that they are part of a group and that being thoughtful and cooperative benefits both themselves and the entire group. In this construction, the group is more than a collection of individual children. Individuals matter, but group needs may supercede the needs of the individual. By including the construct of community, we move beyond attachment theory to include a contextual perspective.

In the conclusion of the book, we return to our framing questions and summarize our responses to them. We end with speculations for the future.

ORIGINAL RESEARCH EVIDENCE

Before ending this introduction, we want to provide more information about the participants and procedures of the original research presented in this book. We believe that our statements are only as "true" as the integrity of the research on which they are built. As noted earlier, we used evidence from several different research projects. They are described in what follows.

Children with Difficult Life Circumstances Study

The first data source is a longitudinal study of preschool-age children coping with difficult life circumstances. We spent 3 school years completing intensive observations in three early childhood programs in very different school sites. We selected the programs both because they served children living in difficult life circumstances and because the teachers and program directors were reflective in their efforts to understand and construct positive child-teacher relationships.

Within each school we collected classroom field notes on six occasions in the fall and six more in the spring. Our observers began taking narrative field notes whenever there was child-teacher or child-child conflict and whenever a child broke a classroom rule. The notes continued until the narrative was resolved or until the participants broke contact. We chose to focus on conflict for two reasons: We felt that these interactions are the most troubling for teachers; and the conflict itself is what the children use to test the strength and mettle of a relationship.

At the conclusion of the fall and spring observation periods, the eight children in the classroom (n = 24 across all three sites) who most often appeared in the field notes were observed through use of an observational measure of attachment quality, the Attachment Q-Set (AQS) (Waters, 1990). The AQS was used to categorize children's attachment organizations (Howes & Ritchie, 1999).

Our first school site was a university laboratory school that serves a diverse population of children in prekindergarten through sixth-grade classrooms. Many live in poverty and in neighborhoods characterized by high levels of violence. The mixed-age classroom we used for our observations served children from 5 to 7 years old.

The second school site was a prekindergarten program for children whose families were homeless. These children ranged in age from 4 to 6 years old. They came from primarily monolingual Spanish-speaking families, and the school program was conducted in their home language.

The third school site was a therapeutic preschool serving children age 4 to 6 years. About half the children in this program had been prenatally exposed to drugs. Many had experienced multiple home placements.

Best Practices Project

Our second data source was the Best Practices Project of the National Center for Early Development and Learning, funded by the U.S. Department of Education. As part of this project we asked community leaders and advocates to identify early childhood programs in Los Angeles County that were doing a particularly good job of serving children coping with difficult life circumstances, particularly children of color. In the subsequent 3 years, we conducted case studies in 10 of these programs in order to understand and describe the practices that made the programs successful. In addition to collecting narratives, as described earlier, we completed detailed observations of 70 randomly selected children in these programs using a measure to observe teacher behaviors toward children, the Teacher Involvement Scale (Howes & Stewart, 1987), and the AQS (Waters, 1990).

Classroom Observations Study

The third data source for this volume consists of narratives collected in classrooms serving children from infancy through elementary school in a wide variety of classroom settings across Los Angeles. The teachers and classroom were not preselected for exemplary practices, as were the other data sources. Instead these narratives represent life in urban schools in the late 1990s. Students who were preparing to teach in primary and secondary school were trained to collect narrative observations as described earlier. Two hours of observation were completed for each classroom. Observers completed up to 10 five-minute narratives spaced across the entire observation period. Children were randomly selected to participate in the narratives.

CONCLUSION

In the course of working on this book, we watched many excellent teachers being effective in their interactions with children. We have come to think of these teachers as resilient—they are continuing in a sometimes daunting profession and being effective despite difficult work circumstances, and they are firm and strong in their interactions with children. They believe that structure and consistency positively contribute to children's ability to trust and feel safe. They have high expectations of their students and convey to them a belief that they can succeed. They establish rules of conduct for all classroom participants, and they hold everyone, including themselves, accountable for following them. They also are charismatic in their warmth and enjoyment of the children. They do smile, often, and before the holiday break. We like to see ourselves as participants in the community of learners that includes these teachers. We know that we have learned from them. If we have been successful in writing this book, we will have provided a means for these teachers to communicate with other teachers who work in classrooms with children facing difficult life circumstances.

Understanding Attachment Organizations and Their Role in the Classroom

Part I of this book is most closely tied to a theoretical and research literature in developmental and clinical psychology. Using this literature, we describe different kinds of child–teacher relationships, explore how such relationships develop and change with attention to conflict and emotions, and describe how they are related to classroom learning. We use the narrative collected in classrooms as illustrations of the behaviors and relationships described in the literature. Thus the evidence in this part is research based.

Chapter 1 is primarily concerned with categories of child–teacher relationships. Although attachment relationships are continuous—children trust their caregivers on a range from not at all to completely—we believe that using categorical descriptions of adaptive and maladaptive attachment relationships can help teachers map their own experiences with children onto the attachment construct. We want to caution readers that these descriptions are intended to aid in understanding, not to be used to classify real children.

In Chapter 2 we examine conflict in the classroom. We argue that classrooms can be harmonious when teachers focus on helping children with relationship building and internalizing dispositions toward regulation and control rather than on classroom-management techniques. We present evidence pointing to pathways between child–teacher relationship quality and peer relationships, suggesting that improving child–teacher relationships is critical for reducing both adult–child and child–child conflict.

Finally, in Chapter 3 we explore the assumption that children use their relationships with teachers to organize their classroom learning, and we suggest that older as well as younger children do so. In this chapter we move from a primary focus on child–teacher relationships to include peers as part of the classroom climate and consider the teacher as an organizer of peer interaction as well as an organizer of children's exploration of ideas and materials.

Child-Teacher Attachment Relationships

According to attachment theory, in which we ground our approach to the development of trusting relationships between children and teachers (Bowlby, 1982), all children become attached to their important adult caregivers, including teachers. Furthermore, again according to this theory, every attachment relationship has an organization. Attachment theorists suggest that there are three basic attachment organizations: secure; avoidant insecure; and insecure ambivalent/resistant (Ainsworth, Blehar, Waters, & Wall, 1978). A fourth category, disorganized, describes relationships that are incoherent and fragmented. The optimal attachment organization is a secure one.

When child-teacher attachment relationships are secure, children trust that they can get help from their teacher when they need it. For example, in the narrative that follows, the children turn to their teacher when their inexperience with a climbing toy and lack of physical competence leads to a problem.

> Jenn is on the top of the slide. Maricel is halfway down the slide. Jenn does not know how to wait just the right amount of time to both get her turn on the slide and not run into Maricel.
>
> Jenn lets go with her hands and halfway down the slide runs into Maricel. Both children make surprised noises. The children are now tangled together and appear afraid to move. They turn and look at Teacher Sylvia who is sitting next to the slide. Sylvia stands up and puts a calm hand on each child. She gently lifts Jenn off the slide. Maricel, now free, goes the rest of the way down the slide. Sylvia helps Jenn try again.

The critical behavior in this narrative is that when stuck, the children turned to the teacher for help. We can assume that previous experiences with Teacher Sylvia have led the children to assume that she will help them solve this new problem.

Empirical studies of children from difficult life circumstance—children who have experienced maltreatment, have been prenatally exposed to drugs, live in extreme poverty—find that as many as 80% of these children have insecure rather than secure attachment organizations with their primary caregivers at home (Lyons-Ruth, 1996; Rodning, Beckwith, & Howard, 1991; Sroufe, Egeland, & Kreutzer, 1990). Children with insecure attachment organizations cannot trust adults to keep them safe. Unlike Jenn and Maricel, they do not believe that their teacher will solve the problem.

We begin this chapter with behavior descriptions of children who have insecure child-teacher attachment organizations. These descriptions come from observers using the Attachment Q-Set (Waters, 1990). When researchers use the AQS, they watch classroom interactions and describe what they see using a set of 90 cards, each describing a behavior of children interacting with adults. The behaviors on the cards are predetermined to belong to particular attachment organizations. The scores derived from an observer's sorting of the cards for a particular child can be matched to a specific attachment organization.

The observers have an outsiders' perspective on the classrooms. Their task is to match their observations with the theoretical profiles described in attachment theory. This means that they are making inferences about adult's and children's behaviors and the meaning of the behaviors based on their knowledge of attachment theory.

Teachers, in contrast to observers, have an insiders' perspective on the classroom. When asked to report on child-teacher relationships, they base their perceptions on what it felt like to engage with this or that child. We compared observer and teacher perceptions of the child-teacher relationships of the same children to explore whether there was agreement between outsiders' and insiders' perceptions of relationships. This comparison is described in the last section of this chapter.

CATEGORIES OF INSECURE CHILD-TEACHER ATTACHMENT ORGANIZATION

Attachment theorists have described two attachment organizations associated with insecure relationships: avoidant and ambivalent/resistant; and a disorganized organization (Ainsworth et al., 1978).

Insecure-Avoidant Attachment Organizations

Children with avoidant attachment organizations turn away rather than seek comfort from adults because they have experienced rejection and insensitivity from adults (Ainsworth et al., 1978). Since they expect the adult to reject them, they tend to make "preemptive strikes," acting in a hostile fashion before the adult has an opportunity to be rejecting. Alternatively, they may avoid the adult in order to avoid being rejected. Children with avoidant maternal attachment histories tend to be rated by teachers as high in aggression and passive withdrawal (Renken, Egeland, Marvinney, Mangelsdorf, & Sroufe, 1989). The following narratives illustrate how children with avoidant attachment organizations can be disruptive in the classroom.

Tim is in a therapeutic preschool and classified in our research program as avoidant with his teacher. The teacher-to-child ratio in this program is one teacher for every two children, and there are only eight children in the classroom. Because of the small number of children and large number of adults, during most of the day all parts of the room are open to the children. But in order to help children learn to regulate their impulses and to make choices, for 15 minutes the children are limited to a smaller set of activities. During this morning's activity period, the classroom rule is that children are free to select an activity from the tables, but may not go into other parts of the room. As teachers are physically in close proximity to the activities on the tables, children who would prefer to not engage with and to remain physically away from the teachers do so. Immediately after morning activity time, the entire room is available to children.

> Tim leaves the table area and heads for the dollhouse that is in a part of the room not open to the children during this time. Ms. Rosen picks him up and brings him back. She says, "I'm going to say no. You can stay over here. You can be with us at the puzzle table." Tim stays at the table for about 5 seconds, and then heads back to the dollhouse. Ms. Rosen goes and gets him, talks to him quietly, holds him, and lets him go. Tim keeps looking for circuitous ways to get back to the dollhouse. Ms. Rosen says, "Tim, I'm going to stop you."

Our repeated observations of Tim suggest that he only remains in close proximity to a teacher or classmate when the teachers insist on bringing him back to the group. Left on his own, his actions with materials are repetitive and stereotypical. It is as if he is preoccupied with staying away from others rather than occupied in the learning potential of his isolated activity.

Geovanni is a second grader in a public urban school. Geovanni's behavior with his teacher, Mr. Rodriguez, is suggestive of an avoidant child-teacher relationship. In this narrative we explore two aspects of Geovanni's behaviors. While engaging in routine behavior with peers, Geovanni is aggressive and disruptive. While in class, he does not participate in learning activities and avoids teacher contact.

> Out on the yard Eusebio comes up to Mr. Rodriguez. He is upset and explains, "He hit me. Geovanni was in the bathroom and he hit me like this." Eusebio demonstrated the punch. Mr. Rodriguez says, "When Geovanni

comes out, we'll ask whether there is a problem." When Geovanni comes out of the bathroom he is confronted by Eusebio and Mr. Rodriguez. Geovanni defends himself, claiming that Eusebio had stolen his stall. He turns his back on Mr. Rodriguez and Eusebio and walks away.

Back in the classroom, Mr. Rodriguez hands out the students' weekly work packets, which contain math worksheets. Geovanni sits at his desk, flicking his pencil against the laminated cover of his math journal. He ignores the weekly packet on his desk. He hums and continually flicks his pencil against his math journal. When Mr. Rodriguez moves in his direction, Geovanni freezes and keeps his eyes down, looking at his paper.

Neither Tim nor Geovanni can use their teacher as a resource for learning. Tim is focused on the dollhouse in an isolated area of the room rather than becoming involved with the teacher in a learning activity. Whether walking away, or distracting himself by "flicking" his pencil, or becoming still so his teacher will not comment on his behavior, Geovanni is managing not to engage with Mr. Rodriguez.

Children whose child-teacher attachment organization is avoidant become all too easy for a teacher to ignore. If Ms. Rosen had simply allowed Tim to play in the dollhouse, she would have missed an opportunity not only to engage him in a learning activity, but also to demonstrate that she wants him to be part of the community of children and teachers. Ms. Rosen teaches in a program designed to attend to child-teacher attachment organizations. In this school teachers bring back to the group children who engage in avoidant behaviors.

Mr. Rodriguez has 32 second graders in his class. From his perspective Geovanni is not a problem. Within the classroom he is quiet and in his seat. His behavior in the bathroom was not particularly outrageous. We are concerned that Geovanni was aggressive and then passively withdrew. We wonder how he can focus on his math problems when his attention is directed toward avoiding school activities.

Insecure-Ambivalent/Resistant Attachment Organizations

Children with an ambivalent/resistant attachment organization also do not trust their attachment figure to provide comfort and emotional security. However, in contrast to children with avoidant attachments, their experience of the attachment figure has been inconsistent and thus confusing (Cassidy & Berlin, 1994). Sometimes the adult will be there for them, and other times the adult will withdraw from the child. Children with ambivalent/resistant attachment organization tend to be dependent and hard to comfort. These children may appear to seek comfort and then reject the adult's attempts to provide it. Thus, these children are both "clingy" and difficult. Children with a history of ambivalent/resistant maternal attachment are characterized as fearful and inhibited in exploration with both peers and materials (Cassidy & Berlin, 1994). As the following narrative illustrates, children with ambivalent/resistant attachment organizations can also be disruptive within classrooms. Unlike the child with an avoidant attachment organization, the child with an ambivalent/resistant attachment organization uses disruptive behavior to draw the teacher into interpersonal conflict.

Diego in Ms. Jones's classroom in the therapeutic preschool was classified in our research as having an ambivalent/resistant attachment relationship with his teacher. When this observation begins, Diego is removing the contents of his cubby and tossing them on the floor. He is supposed to be doing an activity at one of the activity tables.

> Ms. Jones says, "Diego, put it in your cubby if you want it, but it doesn't go on the floor." Diego throws something across the room. Ms. Jones says, "Diego, come and get what you dropped. Here it is." Diego continues to escalate his engagement with Ms. Jones, eventually hiding under the table during cleanup time. Ms. Jones says, "Diego, I need you to come out from under the table, or we'll just save stuff for you to clean up later."

Ms. Mercer is a second-grade teacher. In this narrative she is leading a whole-group discussion about the section that the children have just read. Juan's behavior is similar to that of children with ambivalent/resistant organizations.

> Juan is leaning out of his seat, poking and calling to Miguel. Ms. Mercer says sternly, "Juan, fold your hands. Stop talking." Juan sits properly back in his seat. Ms. Mercer turns her attention back to the whole class. Juan frowns at her and stomps his feet loudly. Ms. Mercer again stops the lesson and reprimands Juan.

In these narratives, the teacher's attention to the child's misdeeds led to an escalation of the misbehavior. The child's goal appears to be to engage the teacher, *rather* than to engage in the misbehavior. This is distinct from what occurs in the previous narrative with a child with an avoidant attachment organization in which the child's goal (getting access to the dollhouse; getting out of a peer conflict within the bathroom) did not change as the teacher intervened.

Children with insecure ambivalent/resistant child-teacher attachment organization may also appear as overly dependent on teachers, as in the following narrative showing Linda's preoccupation with her teacher. Instead of focusing on the learning activity, she focuses on testing whether her teacher is really available to help her. This narrative takes place in a third-and-fourth-grade bilingual Spanish-English classroom. Every morning the students write in their journals. Although we are using the English translation here, our observers were English-Spanish bilingual and recorded the narratives in the language of the speaker.

> When the children had just begun writing, Linda stands up and asks Mr. Boyd, her teacher, to come over. He asks her, "Linda, do you need help?" Linda asks him how to spell a word. Mr. Boyd supplies the answer and moves away. Linda remains motionless looking up at Mr. Boyd. Mr. Boyd asks again, "Do you need help?" Linda says, "I can't do this." Mr. Boyd says, "Every morning we write in our journals. Would you like me to sit at the table with you?" He sits down in the seat next to Linda. Linda smiles, sits back into her seat, and resumes writing in her journal.

Linda's behavior in this narrative was more socially acceptable than that of Juan or Diego in the previous narratives, but it too reveals a preoccupation with her child-teacher relationship rather than the learning activity. Her goal also appears to be to engage the teacher, *rather* than to receive academic help. Mr. Boyd appears to understand that Linda wants help with the academics less than she wants some personal attention. When Linda is in close proximity to Mr. Boyd, her anxiety appears to recede, and she can focus on her journal. This day Mr. Boyd was able to easily sit with her. Another day he may be needed by another child. A reflective teacher who is attentive to the importance of child-teacher relationships might find ways to structure the classroom to keep Linda feeling safe. For example, he might try to position Linda next to him before beginning the journal-writing exercise so that she can use his presence as a secure base from which to learn. In the preceding narrative, Linda lost part of her journal-writing time because of her anxiety. Mr. Boyd had to divert his attention from the whole group to Linda. Perhaps if Linda knew that she could count on sitting next to Mr. Boyd, she could start writing at the beginning of the period.

Disorganized Attachment Organizations

Some children with insecure attachment organizations are disorganized as well as insecure (Main & Solomon, 1990). These children's past experiences with attachment figures leave them with no coherent strategies for seeking comfort or security. Children with initial disorganized attachment organizations tend to be hostile, aggressive, and unable to trust adults to care for them or to help them organize their worlds (Lyons-Ruth, 1996). Unlike the children with avoidant organizations who reject the teacher and the children with ambivalent/resistant organizations who engage the teacher in maladaptive ways, children classified as disorganized have no coherent strategies for interacting with the teacher. These children are probably the most confusing of all for teachers because they are the least predictable. The following narrative illustrates the behavior of a child with a disorganized attachment organization as classified by our research.

> It is activity–table time in Ms. Rosen's room. There are several everyday activity tables, and one special activity, pie baking. As the narrative begins, Ms. Rosen and Carolyn are working on the pie. Henry goes to the table and tries to take away Carolyn's job. Ms. Rosen says, "You know, Henry, if you want to do it, you'll have to wait your turn." Henry leaves the table and goes to the dress-up corner. In a few minutes he returns to the pie baking, and throws things off the table. Ms. Rosen says to Henry, "I need that back on the table, so you need to pick it up right now, and put it on the table." Henry twirls and spins across the room. He falls and bumps his head, but does not look to Ms. Rosen for comfort. Ms. Rosen picks Henry up, helps him pick up the things, and says, "Did you bump your head?" Henry says, "Yes." Ms. Rosen continues, "That is what happens sometimes when you fool around. Are you OK?" Henry says, "Yes." Henry goes over to the block area, which is off limits during activity time. While looking at Ms. Rosen, he begins pounding on some pegboards. Ms. Rosen says, "I'm going to say no to that." She then picks up the pegboards and puts them away.

The child's behavior in this narrative is not coherent or organized. Furthermore, it has elements of both an avoidant organization, as when the child bumps his head and does not seek comfort from the teacher, and an ambivalent/resistant organization, as when the child looks to the teacher as he engages in breaking a classroom rule, pounding on the boards. The child also engaged in some out-of-context behavior, twirling and spinning across the room, when asked to conform to the classroom rules. These behaviors often indicate a disorganized attachment organization.

BEHAVIORS ASSOCIATED WITH DIFFERENT CHILD-TEACHER ATTACHMENT ORGANIZATIONS

In one of the largest observational studies of child-teacher attachment organizations, our observers described child-teacher relationships of 500 children in preschool programs using the AQS (see Howes & Ritchie, 1999, for a full description of the study). The children ranged in age from 3 to

5 years old and were primarily Asian American, African American, or Eurasian. From these data we generated lists of behaviors that correspond to different attachment organizations. We provide them here as an aid to observing children and teachers in classrooms, reminding readers that these lists are *not* intended to be used to classify children.

AVOIDANT INSECURE

- Children are more interested in the materials provided in the classroom than in the teacher or other children.
- Children do not approach the teacher and stay apart from her, so the teacher can easily lose track of them.
- When the teacher approaches the children, they act as if they do not hear what she says or notice what she does.
- After responding to a teacher request to come near, children quickly leave her side.
- Children do not call out to the teacher to show her something new.
- When the children are hurt or upset, they do not seek out the teacher and move away from her if she moves to comfort them.

RESISTANT INSECURE

- Children are irritable and fussy with the teacher with no apparent cause.
- Children often cry, and they cry hard and are difficult to console.
- Children resist classroom routines such as cleaning up.
- If the primary teacher attempts to leave the room, the children cling to her and then continue to cry after she leaves.
- Every bump or scratch is an occasion for tears.
- Children easily become angry and frustrated when they cannot accomplish a task
- Children are demanding and impatient with the teacher and are not satisfied with her attempts to respond to them.
- Children act as if they expect the teacher to interfere in their activities.
- Children are rough with the teacher and bump, kick, or scratch her as they engage in play with her.
- Children cry to get the teacher to do what they want her to do.

SECURE

- Children accept comfort if they are hurt or upset.
- Children mold their bodies to the teacher if she is holding them or gently touch the teacher as they play with her.

- Children spontaneously hug the teacher.
- If children are afraid or upset the teacher can hold them and children relax.
- Children readily share their activities with the teacher, going to her with new things and welcoming her entrance into their play.
- Children check back with the teacher throughout the day.
- Children ask for help if they need it.
- Children are lighthearted and playful with the teacher.
- Children easily follow the suggestions and directions of the teacher.
- Children act sorry or ashamed if the teacher speaks firmly to them and stop misbehavior when teacher says to stop.
- Transitions within the day are smooth and easy for these children.
- Children are happy to see the teacher at the beginning of the day.

ASSOCIATIONS BETWEEN OBSERVER AND TEACHER PERCEPTIONS OF CHILD-TEACHER RELATIONSHIPS

In addition to including the researchers' observations in our study (Howes & Ritchie, 1999), we asked the teachers to assess their own relationships with the children using the Student Teacher Rating Scale (STRS) (Pianta, Steinberg, & Rollins, 1997). This measures classifies teacher-perceived child-teacher relationships as close, conflictual, or dependent (Pianta et al., 1997). As we have described earlier in this chapter, the child with a close and positive child-teacher relationship can use the support provided by this relationship to explore and master school learning tasks. In contrast, the child with a conflictual child-teacher relationship cannot use that relationship as a base of support and may be anxious or fearful about going to school. Furthermore, a difficult child-teacher relationship may interfere with the child's attention to the school environment and interfere with or distract the child from learning and achievement. A third feature of child-teacher relationships is dependency. Clinging and immature rather than close and positive reciprocated interactions characterize a dependent child-teacher relationship. A child who is overly dependent on the teacher is unlikely to explore the school environment or relationships with peers (Birch & Ladd, 1997). Therefore, as with a conflictual child-teacher relationship, a dependent child-teacher relationship is expected to interfere with school adjustment and achievement.

When the teachers in our study had completed Pianta's STRS on their children, we compared their ratings to those of our observers. Our researchers' classrom observations found only 30% percent of the 500 child-teacher relationships to be secure. Another 24% of the relationships were classified as avoidant, and 7% as resistant. The rest could not be classified and may have been disorganized. We found that children categorized as unclassifiable, resistant, and avoidant in their child-teacher relationship organization had higher teacher-reported conflict scores than children categorized as secure or near secure.

Our observers and the teachers who participated in this study did not confer with one another about child-teacher relationships. Still, the relationships that researchers observed to be insecure were described by the teachers as difficult—high in conflict. This is important confirmation that the observers' conclusions were consistent with the teachers' viewpoints.

This study also is important in our larger goal of working with teachers to help them understand and explore child-teacher relationships in a sophisticated manner. We are particularly interested that the teachers appear to perceive little difference between their relationships with children whom we classified as secure and their relationships with children who could not be classified. In our view, the children classified as secure trusted their teachers, while the children we could not classify were compliant and well behaved but not trusting. Perhaps their ability to cooperate with their teachers masks their more distrusting behaviors. Helping teachers learn the difference between good behavior and trust could allow them to think carefully about how to help these children move from compliance to warmth. In future chapters we will explore ways that teachers can enhance their relationships with their students.

SUMMARY

We assume that all children become attached to their important adult caregivers, including teachers, and that every attachment relationship has an organization. We used our narrative records to illustrate several different attachment organization characteristics of our participant children who cope with difficult life circumstances. Children with insecure child-teacher attachment organizations appear unable to use the teacher to help them learn in the classroom. Instead, their distrustful child-teacher relationships interfere with their ability to learn.

There are two subcategories of insecure attachment organizations. The behaviors characteristic of these organizations are quite distinct. Children with insecure avoidant attachment relationship organizations tend to avoid child-teacher interaction, but are often aggressive and disruptive with peers. Children with insecure resistant attachment relationship organizations, in contrast, appear to seek unpleasant child-teacher interactions. Sometimes, these interactions are hostile or contentious, and sometimes the child is over-dependent—clingy and whining. Children who fit the third classification, disorganized, are probably the most perplexing for teachers because they exhibit no coherent strategies for interacting with the teacher. At times these children are demanding and disruptive, at other times avoiding.

Teachers vary in their attentiveness to child-teacher relationships and in their ability to reflect on the patterns of their interactions with children. However, in a large study of teachers in preschool programs, we found that teacher ratings of their relationships with children were often consistent with those of observers. However, these data also suggest that some children who were identified by observers as having difficulty with their child-teacher relationships were not seen as problematic by their teachers. The observers described these children as conforming to the class rules, but acting as if they did not trust their teacher. The teachers described these same children as having a positive relationship and not having behavior problems. We are concerned that these findings may indicate that teachers are too preoccupied with acting-out children to notice quiet children who also have trouble in their classroom.

2

Child–Teacher Relationships and Harmonious Interactions

In the preceding chapter we saw that children who have insecure or problematic relationships with their teachers were more likely to engage in conflict. In this chapter we want to focus on acrimonious interactions because this kind of interaction disrupts the learning of the child involved and at times the entire classroom. Acrimonious interactions can involve conflicts between teachers and children or between children and children. They are often marked by verbal or physical aggression, disregard for classroom rules of conduct, or disputes over materials. We prefer to call them acrimonious rather than conflictual interactions because in these episodes children introduce disruptive behaviors and teachers can respond by escalating or deescalating behaviors. The goal of teachers who wish to maximize harmonious interactions in the classroom is to keep acrimonious interactions from becoming conflicts that disrupt learning.

In the following narrative a novice first-grade teacher, Ms. Knott, is unable to conduct a learning activity because of the conflictual interactions between her students and between her students and herself. At the beginning of the narrative, the children are finishing up a writing assignment. Their teacher wants them to come together for story reading. This is an "everyday" transition; the class has been together for 3 months and might be expected to move smoothly from one activity to the next.

> Ms. Knott asks children to put their papers in the box and return to their chairs for a story. Children move all over the classroom, talking loudly. Many congregate around the box, some put papers away then move around the room, only a few return to their desks, and several never get close to the box. Ms. Knott yells at the students, "What's going on? Why are you making so much noise? You wanted to read the story!" Ms. Knott directs individual children back to their seats by name.

Ten minutes pass before Ms. Knott is reading a book to the whole class. All the students are sitting at their desks (in a U shape) with the teacher standing at the opening of the desks. Many students are unable to see the pictures. They squirm in their seats and talk to their neighbors. Ms. Knott gets upset with them and tells them she knows it's hard to see, but if they had been able to control themselves and not get so loud on the rug, then they could be sitting on the rug instead.

Then Ms. Knott appears to change her mind and gets out a blanket for the class to sit on. The children move to the blanket. Ms. Knott rearranges them all, with the taller children in back so that everyone can see.

Ten more minutes have passed. Ms. Knott begins reading the story aloud again. One of the students, Kenya, is fingering her jacket. Her neighbor, Caro, interrupts Ms. Knott to report that Kenya just hit her. Ms. Knott stops reading. She tells Kenya to move back to her seat. She asks Kenya to tell Caro she's sorry. Kenya says it was accidental. Ms. Knott says, "If you really mean it, tell her you're sorry." Kenya says, "I told her I was sorry," and folds her arms across her chest. A chorus of other girls says, "Kenya didn't say she was sorry." Ms. Knott ignores the girls and begins the story again.

It is easy to blame the teacher in this narrative. Was her story reading boring? Should she have had all 20 children move so many times in a short period? Why was her class so unable to make transitions? Why did she yell at her students? Why did she blame them when they could not see the pictures in the book? An alternative reading of this narrative suggests a frustrated teacher who wants her students to like her, who wants her children to get along, and who believes that she is paying attention to the social relationships within her classroom ("She asks Kenya to tell Caro she's sorry"). We believe that Ms. Knott engaged in conflict rather than deescalating the situation ("Ms. Knott gets upset with them and tells them she knows it's hard to see, but if they had been able to control themselves and not get so loud on the rug, then they could be sitting on the rug instead"). What could have Ms. Knott done to move the acrimonious interaction away from conflict and toward harmonious interactions and learning?

In this chapter we provide guidance for teachers like Ms. Knott who want to increase harmonious interactions in their classrooms. In order for classroom interaction to be harmonious, there must be agreement on the rules of conduct. By rules of conduct we mean the explicit and implicit rules for which behaviors and interactions are permitted and forbidden in classrooms. For example, referring to the narrative about Carolyn in the Introduction, the rule of conduct was, Only one person talks at a time during circle time. In Chapter 1 the rule in the example about Jenn was, Only one child may be sliding at a time; and in the narrative about Juan, Children do not poke one another.

This chapter, like the previous one, draws on research for its evidentiary base. Again we use our classroom narratives for illustration of research-based knowledge rather than drawing on them for evidence. The argument we make is a complex one and in some ways goes against "conventional wisdom" about teaching. An analysis of the narratives collected in our third data source—the classroom observation study—suggests that most teachers who appeared concerned with changing social climates and creating communities of learners used direct instruction and behaviorist-based classroom-management techniques.

BELIEFS ABOUT TEACHING AND LEARNING

The first-grade teacher in the following narrative is representative of these teachers. She appears to believe that teaching rules of conduct prevents conflict. She tells the children that if the classroom is harmonious, all the children can learn.

> Ms. Headrick is going over the rules of the class. She asks everyone, "What does it mean to be the best class?" Regina raises her hand and answers, "Pay attention. Listen. Sit nicely." Ms. Headrick writes those answers on the whiteboard. Leslie answers, "We share and care." Brianna, who has her hand up, waits until she is called upon and answers, "Don't speak out." Angel says, "Don't talk back." Ezrae says, "Let other people talk." All the answers are placed on the whiteboard. Ms. Headrick says, "Those are great ways to be the best class."
>
> Ms. Headrick is at the front of the class. She asks the students, "What are Five Star Days?" The students respond by waving their hands. She calls on Brittney, "They are when we be the best we can and do what we came for." Ms. Headrick replies, "That's right, Brittney. What did we come to school for, class?" The class chants out in unison, "To LEARN!" Matthew, who had been poking at a spot on the carpet, didn't speak. Ms. Headrick says, "I didn't hear you, Matthew, why did we come here today?" He looks up at her and says, "To learn."
>
> Ezrae continues answering Ms. Headrick's question about rules. He says, "Let other people talk." Klivae is sitting on the opposite side of the room. It appears as if he is not paying attention. Ms. Headrick asks, "Klivae, what did Ezrae say?" Klivae does not respond. She then says, "Robert, can you help Klivae remember what Ezrae said?" Robert says, "He said to let other people have a turn."

The question-response format used by Ms. Headrick may produce children who could do well on a test of basic social-behavior skills, but who may not necessarily have the internalized dispositions from which harmonious interaction is derived (Stipek, Feiler, Daniels, & Milburn, 1995).

In this chapter we argue that this particular conventional wisdom about teaching is contrary to the research evidence. We provide evidence from research that

- Children comply with rules of conduct because they have internalized dispositions to regulate and control their emotions and behavior.
- The theoretical approaches of Vygotsky and Rogoff to teaching and learning are more successful in helping children to internalize these dispositions toward regulation and control than is direct instruction.
- Children's development of internalized dispositions toward regulation and control is dependent on their child-adult relationship quality.
- Achieving harmonious interactions in the classroom requires attention to the internalized dispositions, children's behaviors, adult behaviors, and child-adult relationships.

The following narrative illustrates an alternative approach to that of Ms. Headrick. Ms. Mack is working with her first graders to construct classroom rules of conduct.

Ms. Mack says, "Everybody, put your journals away," and tells the children it's time for a class meeting, mentioning that they haven't had a class meeting in a long time. Ms. Mack talks about how she's noticed a lot of talking lately. She says, "You have all gotten to be very good friends and that's good, but that means you have lots to say to each other."

Ms. Mack talks about how the problem is that they're talking even when they should be listening and paying attention to others. She then asks the class what they'll be responsible for after the winter holiday, and the class responds that they'll have to do the calendar on their own. Ms. Mack says she's worried that some children won't know how to do it because they haven't been paying attention and they've been busy talking.

Ms. Mack says that they have happy and sad faces and they put names in the sad faces when children are not remembering to be quiet and good listeners. Ms. Mack asks what more they can do to help everyone be better listeners. Ms. Mack says one person's name was on the board both yesterday and today, so the names on the board don't seem to be working.

The children all ask who it was who had their name on the board both days, but Ms. Mack says it doesn't matter who it was because all children have their names on the board at some point.

One child suggests that they use a contraption on children who are talking. Ms. Mack asks him if he means something like a mousetrap, then says that they don't want to hurt anybody. He tries to explain some more and suggests a rubber ducky that they could squirt at children who are talking, but Ms. Mack says that they don't want to squirt children inside either.

Another child suggests that Ms. Mack just ignore the children who are being loud. Ms. Mack explains that it's really distracting to have others talking, so ignoring them is too hard.

Another child suggests that Ms. Mack talk to the parents of children who talk. Ms. Mack discussed how they might do that (i.e., when children are being dropped off/picked up, by phone, by letter) and says that's an option.

Another child suggests that they move their seats around. Ms. Mack asks, "Do you mean switch rug spots around?" and says that that option might work.

Another child suggests that Ms. Mack put a box on the board, and when children are talking, she put a number in the box. When the number gets up to 3, all the children have to put their heads on their desks. Ms. Mack says that that is an option and asks if there are any other suggestions.

Ms. Mack says, "Let's vote. So far we talked about three options: talking to parents, putting a box on the board and having children put their heads down when the talking gets too loud, and changing rug spots." An overwhelming majority of children chose changing rug spots.

Ms. Mack suggests one problem with this option. She says they don't have rug spots during calendar. The children suggest that they have rug spots for calendar, too. Ms. Mack agrees.

They decide that they're going to try to rearrange rug spots before recess. Ms. Mack tells the children to sit on their rug spots, and as children are sitting, she asks how they should change. One child says, "Cooper." Ms. Mack says, "Yes. Cooper's always looking to the back so I think she needs to sit in the back." Cooper and Benedicta switch places.

Ms. Mack asks who else has problems talking. Many children offer up themselves, and many children switch places, with Ms. Mack occasionally vetoing possible options. After moving quite a few students around, children are still saying that they are next to their friends. Ms. Mack says that because they're all such good friends they can't get away from sitting next to a friend, but they want to try not to sit next to a best-best friend. Some children still protest, but Ms. Mack says, "Let's try what we have now and see how it works." She suggests that they can always try something else if this arrangement doesn't work.

Work on teaching and learning based on the theoretical principles of Vygotsky suggests that this kind of teaching may be particularly advantageous for children's development of internalized behaviors, including their motivation to learn (Rogoff, 1990; Stipek et al., 1995). Ms. Mack may eventually use some of the same strategies to prevent conflict and disruption as

Ms. Headrick. Certainly some of the "tools," including sad and happy faces, and names or a box on the board, sound very familiar to people who have been reading manuals on classroom management. What makes this narrative distinctive is the joint participation of the children and the teacher in the construction of the rules for conduct. Ms. Mack may veto a rule or set of rules. She clearly does not like the idea of the "contraption," and she does limit the voting choices. But the students are active participants in the decision. We find the enthusiasm with which the children figure out how to arrange themselves on the rug particularly noteworthy. Unfortunately, we did not revisit Ms. Mack and her class to see what happened next. We suspect that she continued to have the entire classroom evaluate how these new strategies were working. Her teaching strategy is consistent with the development of internalized dispositions toward regulation and control. When children have developed these internalized dispositions, they are better able to cooperate. In the following sections of this chapter we will define internalized dispositions and review the research on their development.

INTERNALIZED DISPOSITIONS TOWARD
REGULATION AND CONTROL

Internalized dispositions are children's capacity to, on their own and without fear of noncompliance, control and appropriately express their emotions and behavior. In other words, it is the ability of children to behave with "gracious manners," to be kind to others, to engage in harmonious interaction because they want to do so. These internalized behaviors or dispositions toward regulation and control, rather than specific social skills, are associated with harmonious interactions within classrooms. Children who are able to strike a balance between their own desires and interests and those of the other children and teachers are able to regulate and control their emotions and impulses (Eisenberg et al., 1999; Fabes et al., 1999).

Three internalized dispositions are associated with the regulation and control of emotions and behaviors. These highly interrelated internalized dispositions that underlie harmonious interaction are inhibitory control, effortful control, and emotional regulation.

Inhibitory Control

Inhibitory control, sometimes called self-control, is the ability to distinguish between behavior that is appropriate and permitted by the rules of social conduct within a context and activities that are impermissible, and to comply with what is expected (Crockenberg & Litman, 1990; Kochanska, Aksan,

& Koenig, 1995; Kochanska, Murray, & Coy, 1997). Children with appropriate inhibitory control who are enrolled in classrooms that do not permit talking to peers are able to be quiet. Such children enrolled in classrooms that encourage peer collaboration are able to keep their voices low, to not interrupt, and to otherwise follow the rules of conduct for that classroom. In both classroom environments, children with appropriate inhibitory control will spontaneously or willingly comply with teacher directions with little pressure from the teacher.

Toddlers are famous for their struggles with inhibitory control:

> Eliza looks with interest at Martha's ponytail. She reaches her hand out toward it. Her teacher says, "Remember—gentle touches, Eliza; you would like to touch Martha's hair, but it hurts Martha when you pull on her ponytail."

But older children continue to have trouble with inhibitory control. This narrative was collected in a first-grade classroom:

> Emily is writing out words. Bernice gets out of her seat and stands next to Emily. She says a couple of sentences to Emily, but Emily doesn't respond. She reaches for a little ponytail hanging down Emily's neck, saying she likes the "thing hanging down." Emily says abruptly, "Don't pull it," and pulls back her clenched hand, apparently preparing to hit Bernice, then sees me [the observer] watching and stops with her hand still held slightly in the air.

Children can, of course, comply out of fear or anxiety and not from an internalized disposition toward harmonious rather than conflictual interaction. Kochanska uses the term "committed compliance" to distinguish between children who are exercising inhibitory control from an internalized disposition toward cooperation and children who are behaving but have not internalized control (Kochanska et al., 1995). As we will discuss shortly, the pathway to committed compliance may be different from the pathway to externalized control.

Effortful Control

Effortful control is children's ability to sustain their focused attention and inhibit imminent actions (Eisenberg, Fabes, Nyman, Bernzweig, & Pinneulas, 1994; Gunnar, Trout, de Haan, Pierce, & Stansbury, 1997). Researchers often define effortful control with reference to children's games, in particular, Simon Says and Red Light, Green Light. In both games children exercise effortful control as they stop immediately when the leader says "red light," or listen carefully to the leader say "Simon says don't skip."

Effortful control is particularly important in peer interaction. Young children often get into conflicts when they are engrossed in an activity that is incompatible with that of a peer. For example, if Josie is intent on making a pattern with the small blocks that involves red triangles, green arrows, and yellow pentangles, she is not necessarily thinking about the fact that Marcy is constructing a pattern with black squares, purple circles, and also yellow pentangles. When there are not enough yellow pentangles, effortful control is helpful to both Josie and Marcy. If the girls have acquired effortful control, they can engage in constructive coping (Eisenberg et al., 1994). Constructive coping is behavior that is not hostile—a verbal self-defense or a demand, such as "Hey, that's mine and I need it"—as opposed to nonconstructive coping, which is hostile and out of control—yelling, screaming, stomping feet, or retaliating (for example, if Marcy were to throw Josie's pieces on the floor and grab the yellow ones).

Emotional Regulation

Emotional regulation is the ability to modulate emotional responsiveness and act competently and effectively in emotionally evocative situations (Eisenberg & Fabes, 1992; Fabes et al., 1999). Emotional regulation becomes particularly important when classroom events evoke negative emotions—anger, distress, shame.

In this narrative, Jose has joined this second-grade classroom just 3 days after emigrating from Mexico to Los Angeles. Jose speaks and understands only Spanish. Because of a political atmosphere that mandates an English-only policy in California schools, Jose is taught only in English. As the narrative begins, the teacher is administering a spelling test (in English). What may seem on the surface to be a routine classroom activity evokes distress and shame for Jose.

> Jose watches the other children and follows their example. He clears his desk of papers and places a piece of paper directly in the middle of the desk. He writes numbers down the side of the paper. The teacher says, "Number 1, the spelling word is *you*." Jose looks at his paper and does not write. The teacher continues. "Number 2, *we*," and so on. Jose stares across the room looking uncomfortable. The teacher finishes the test. She moves around the room, collecting the tests. Jose erases all the numbers he had written on his paper. He looks up at the teacher. He hands the teacher the blank piece of paper, sighs, and puts his head down on his desk.

In this instance, Jose's behavior was certainly conducive to the learning of other children. He did regulate his emotions. However, this narrative raises other questions. Jose's ability to regulate his emotions of shame and frustration may not have earned him attention by the teacher and will likely set him up for similar situations that evoke distress and shame. It is important to distinguish between the modulation and the expression of emotion. There would have been a different ending to this narrative if Jose had expressed his emotions as well as modulated them. We are not recommending a different pattern of behavior for Jose. His ability to modulate his emotions may make him a more likable student. We wish that the teacher had noticed Jose's distress and had changed the interaction to one that did not evoke distress and shame.

Exuberance

Emotional regulation and effortful control are especially important for the temperamentally exuberant child within a classroom environment with rules such as "walk, not run," "wait our turn," and "sit still in circle time." Exuberant children, more often boys than girls, tend to be socially active, aggressive, and interested in trying all sorts of new things, right now (Gunnar et al., 1997). Exuberant children who can control and modulate their emotions are highly valued as classmates, while those who are less able to engage in emotional regulation are viewed as difficult (Rubin, Coplan, Fox, & Calkins, 1995).

Shakir (age 8) is an exuberant child. In this narrative he struggles to contain his exuberance in school.

Shakir is in the middle of taking his spelling test. The word he and the class are told to write is *lick*. Shakir sounds out the word and as he writes it down makes licking sounds and motions with his tongue.

Lyle (age 6), in contrast, is not successful at containing his exuberance.

The class is working on vocabulary development. They are looking at snowmen and talking about their different features. Ms. Brandt is asking the children a variety of questions. "Who knows what color this snowman is?" She looks for a raised hand and calls on Enid. Enid begins to answer in a quiet voice. She cannot be heard because Lyle yells out, "WHITE." Ms. Brandt says, "Lyle, I know you know the answer, but other children get to have a turn. Now Enid, what color in the snowman?" Enid answers and Ms. Brandt moves on, pointing to the snowman's nose. "Now, what is this part of the snowman called?" Once again she looks for a raised hand, but before she can call on anyone, Lyle once again yells out "NOSE."

Lyle is clearly enjoying himself. He is proud and excited to know the answers and does not see himself as interrupting or rude. The dilemma for Shakir and Lyle's teachers is how to enjoy and enhance the boys' sheer joy in learning without shaming them or allowing their behavior to interfere with the learning of the other children. As we discuss later in this chapter, teacher behaviors that help children form mutually reciprocal child-teacher relationships include being emotionally responsive and coaching to help with emotional regulation. These strategies may be particularly effective with exuberant children who are excited about learning; they may be less effective if exuberant children come to equate school with harsh and restrictive behavior.

LINKING CHILDREN'S INTERNALIZED DISPOSITIONS TO HARMONIOUS INTERACTIONS

In the previous section we described children's internalized dispositions toward regulation and control. In this section we link these internalized dispositions to harmonious interactions. Are children who have developed internalized dispositions toward regulation and control of emotions and impulses more likely to engage in harmonious interactions? When we consider the research evidence, the answer is a strong yes. For example, in a series of studies, Eisenberg and Fabes report that children who score higher on measures of control and regulation of emotions and behavior are better liked by other children and more likely to respond to others in socially competent ways (Eisenberg et al., 1999; Fabes et al., 1999).

In order to examine the links between children's internalized dispositions and harmonious interaction with others, we must make these assumptions:

- Harmonious interaction develops from the contributions of both partners in the interaction—children and their teacher or children and their peers.
- The behaviors that children contribute to interactions are a result of their internalized dispositions for regulation and control, their social skills, and prior history with attachment relationships.
- The social skills of the partner, be it a teacher or a peer, also contribute to the nature of the interaction.

Thus, in order to explore links between children's internalized dispositions and behaviors they use in harmonious interaction with peers and teachers, the contributions of children, teachers, and peers must all be considered. First, let us focus on children's behaviors and then in the following section consider adult contributions to interactions.

Links Between Internalized Dispositions and Children's Behavior

As noted earlier, in general, children who are observed or rated to have higher levels of internalized dispositions toward control and regulation are also observed or rated as having more behavior compatible with harmonious interaction. Children in elementary and middle school classrooms who are unable to inhibit their impulses and regulate their emotions typically have a history of behavior problems extending back to preschool (Coie & Dodge, 1997; DeKlyen, Biernbaum, Speltz, & Greenberg, 1998). Likewise, children with more effortful control are seen as less aggressive and more socially competent and as having fewer behavior problems (Rothbart, Ahadi, & Hershey, 1994).

Harmonious interaction is most likely to occur when children are socially competent; that is, children who genuinely like and respect the others in their classroom—teachers and children—and who assist in solving conflicts, helping others, and sharing ideas and materials. These children engage in responsive and reciprocated interactions that address the goals and desires of all participants and their enjoyment of classroom activities. In other words, the ideal child.

Socially competent children score very high on measures of internalized dispositions toward control and regulation of emotions (Putallaz & Sheppard, 1992). They can display emotions that are appropriate to the context and group norms and can negotiate between their own desires and interests and those of other interaction partners.

In this playground observation, we watched Danielle, who at 6 years old is taller and heavier than many of her classmates, display emotions appropriate to the context and negotiate a potentially hurtful situation. Our playground informant explained that the boys had been teasing Danielle by calling her Lilybodchik for several weeks.

> Aki yells at Danielle, "Lilybodchik!" Danielle gets up from the bench and starts to chase Aki. Danielle laughs and says, "You're asking for it." Anthony calls out, "Lilybodchik." Anthony is shorter than the majority of the children. Danielle growls, "Grr, you're probably going to be my size when you get to high school."

In a context that demanded high levels of control and regulation (teasing and running with size and strength disparity), Danielle's appropriate emotional display and behavior diffused a potentially conflictual situation despite Aki's and Anthony's acrimonious behaviors.

Socially competent children can modulate their own emotional responses so that when they engage with others they behave in ways that contribute to positive or constructive social interaction. They are friendly. They help others. They express affection. And they defend others. They are less likely to make other children cry, to tease, or to be a bully (Fabes et al., 1999).

In the following narrative, a 4-year-old child makes another child cry by teasing her. Amanda acts to defend the child who had her feelings hurt. In this narrative Amanda is displaying social competence.

> Ashley, Alexis, and Dylan are seated at a table eating their breakfast. Alexis begins a conversation by saying, "I'm beautiful." Ashley then says, "I'm beautiful too." Alexis responds to Ashley's comment by saying, "No you're not. You're not beautiful." Ashley makes a face and shouts, "You're not allowed to say that! I'm pretty! You are wrong, Alexis! I am pretty! My grandma and grandpa do think I'm pretty!" Ashley then pushes Alexis. Dylan then says to Ashley, "You're not pretty at all." Ashley starts crying. A few minutes later, Amanda, who was sitting close by, approaches Ashley and says, "I think you are beautiful."

It is important to note that definitions of social competence include both the modulation and the expression of emotion. When in classrooms we observe children with difficult life circumstances, we often see that their hard life experiences enter the classroom with them. This means that negative emotions as well as positive ones are expressed there. The tasks for teachers are to attend to the real feelings of the children *and* to not let learning in the classroom be interrupted. The following narrative occurred in a first-grade classroom. Ms. Highland, the teacher, is clearly in touch with the feelings of her students and intends to make the classroom a place for learning. In this narrative she is paying attention to their nonverbal bids for attention and help and is validating their sadness and distress. She then relies on the social skills of another child to draw Colin into the classroom community.

> Colin begins to quietly cry while in his seat. He appears very distressed. Ms. Highland asks, "Are you still sick, Colin? You're still not feeling well yet, huh? You were in the hospital, weren't you?" Colin nods his head. She then leads him over to the circular table, where he sits down in the chair next to Lillian. Lillian turns to Colin and puts her arm around his shoulder. Slowly, Colin stops crying.

Gender. The links between harmonious interaction and internalized dispositions toward regulation and control may be stronger for boys than for girls. Boys, for reasons of biological differences, socialization differences, or both, may, more than girls, have difficulty with regulation and control of emotions and impulses (Maccoby, 1998). For example, boys are more likely than girls to engage in high-arousal, rough-and-tumble play. The boys who can make a smooth transition between rough-and-tumble to calm play are more popular with both sex peers than the boys who find this difficult. Similarly, boys who can constructively cope with anger are rated as more socially competent (Eisenberg et al., 1994). Therefore, teachers may need to use different strategies or be differently attentive to boys than to girls. These differential behaviors need, however, to be applied in the context of creating a classroom community free of gender bias.

Context. Some classroom contexts require more internalized dispositions than others. For example, circle time in preschool requires more regulation and control than does outdoor-play time. Other contexts that require regulation and control include transitions, in other words, stopping one thing and starting another. The following narrative illustrates individual differences in children's ability to handle transitions. Ms. Leo has planned a literacy activity that includes second graders silently reading a few sentences, calling on one child to read the selection aloud, and then a group discussion of the meaning of the selection. As is not uncommon in urban schools, there were not enough books for everyone, so children were to sit in pairs. Kenny and Salina are siting side by side and sharing a copy when this narrative begins.

> Kenny and Salina stop their silent reading before Ms. Leo asks for the next person to read aloud. Each takes a ruler that had been left over from the preceding math exercise. They have an imaginary sword fight, complete with whispering, fighting sounds, and making faces. Ms. Leo is working with a student on the other side of the room. When she turns around, Kenny and Salina stop dueling. Ms. Leo again turns her attention to a struggling student. Kenny and Salina pretend to use their "swords" to cut up cardboard boxes on their desks. They make sound effects and grimace. Ms. Leo looks their way and both turn to their reading. Another student, Antonio, gets up from the next table and wraps his arms around Kenny in a type of wrestling move. Kenny says loudly, "Get off me, man. What's up with you, Pikachu-man?" Salina says, " Pikachu-man? No, he's a weak–a–chu man." Kenny and Salina laugh. Ms. Leo says, "OK, now you are talking. I assume you are finished," and calls on a student to read aloud.
>
> Later during the same exercise Destiny and Robert silently read together. As Robert reads aloud, Destiny plays with an eraser. When Ms. Leo asks what will happen next in the story, she quickly raises her hand. When called on, she says, "The Headless Horseman will get a pumpkin with a face on it and throw it at Ichabod." Ms. Leo repeats this prediction and writes it on the overhead. Destiny and Robert read together again. When they turn the

page, Robert says, "He doesn't have a head," and points to the picture. Destiny replies "He's the Headless Horseman, what do you think!"

This sequence of tasks, reading silently while adjusting reading pace to that of a peer, waiting until the teacher changes the task, being quiet during the read-aloud portion, and listening and responding during discussion demands regulation and control. Salina, Antonio, and Kenny do not appear to have sufficient internalized dispositions toward control and regulation to sustain learning in this way. Perhaps in a different context, if they each had a book, they could complete the task. Destiny acts a little bored when Robert reads, but she is able to attend and contribute to the discussion. When she is bored, her behavior is contained and does not interfere with others and, we presume, her own attention to the learning activity, as demonstrated by her comment during the discussion. If the teacher was able to adjust the context so that it required less internalized control and regulation, Kenny, Salina, and Antonio might have been able to do the task.

In this section we have argued that children who have higher levels of internalized dispositions toward regulation and control—who are able to modulate, monitor, and appropriately control their emotions and behaviors—are more likely to engage in behaviors that enhance harmonious interactions. We suggest that this may be more important for boys than girls, and we note that for all children the classroom context can make it harder or easier to regulate and control emotions and behavior.

Links Between Children's Internalized Dispositions and Adult's Behavior

We turn now to the adult's role in harmonious interactions by examining links between children's internalized dispositions and adult behavior. In infants, internalized dispositions are highly related to temperament, biological variations in their dispositions. By early childhood, children have negotiated the expression of temperament with the adults and other children in their lives (Rothbart & Bates, 1998), and children's expression of internalized dispositions are a product of previous experiences with adults and peers. By late preschool and school age, children's ability to engage in socially adaptive and competent interaction depends on their acquisition of regulation and control and on their relatedness to adults and peers (Egeland, Carlson, & Sroufe, 1993; Wyman et al., 1999). Because the goal of socialization is to promote children's self-control and cooperation and the management of aggressive and antisocial impulses (Maccoby & Martin, 1986), most children discontinue their problematic behavior as they get older. However, some children who have problems with impulse control, effortful control, and emotional regulation as young children become adolescent children with behavior problems (Coie & Dodge, 1997). For these children, experiences with adults and peers did not facilitate their social adaptation.

As one would expect, most of the research on socialization of internalized dispositions toward regulation and control is based on studies of children with their parents. However, as discussed in Chapter 1 and elaborated on throughout the book, many of the same processes that occur in child-parent interaction also are found in child-teacher interaction.

In considering the findings from studies of links between adult behaviors and children's internalized dispositions, it is important to note that we cannot really tell if the behavior of the adult caused that of the child. Some studies, however, have followed children over a number of years, so in these cases we can say that earlier behavior of adults is linked to later behavior of children.

Another caution related to drawing conclusions from research on socialization is that the particular strategies and behaviors used in constructing relationships are dependent on the particular context (Harwood, Miller, & Irizarry, 1995; van IJzendoorn & Sagi, 1999). However, the underlying dimensions of secure or insecure attachment relationships are similar across race, culture, gender, and social class (Posada et al., 1995; van IJzendoorn & Sagi, 1999). Therefore, the construction of relationships rests on both universal principles and contextually particular components. We can infer that prosocial behaviors are linked to prosocial interactions that in turn contribute to a climate of harmonious interaction. But the particular strategies used by adults and children will depend on the race, culture, gender, and social-class context of the interactions and relationships. The conclusions in much of the research linking adult practices and children's behaviors are based on studies of white, middle-class mother-child interactions in families with fathers present. Therefore, the strategies identified may be particular to that context. We draw on this research because, although limited, it points to universal principles that can be adapted to particular teachers, children, and classrooms. By examining these strategies in diverse contexts we can move to differentiating universal from specific strategies.

Attachment Relationships, Internalized Control, and Mutually Reciprocated Relationships. Expression and response to emotion are integral to the development of attachment relationships and to the socialization of internalized dispositions toward regulation and control (Cassidy, 1994). Very young children typically are distressed when caregivers are perceived as unavailable. The responses of the adult to the child's distress in the context of separation are important in the construction of variations in relationship quality. When caregivers are available and comforting, children are calmed and use their secure relationship with the caregiver to organize, modulate, and regulate their emotions. When children's relationship histories include caregivers who are chronically unavailable or rejecting, children live with the fear of being left vulnerable and alone. As described in Chapter 1, a response to a chronic emotional state of fear and distress is anxious vigilance, characteristic of children with insecure resistant attachment organizations (Cassidy & Berlin, 1994). Another response to unavailable, rejecting caregivers is anger. Children who have avoidant attachment organizations are often angry and aggressive toward caregivers (Lyons-Ruth, 1996; Renken et al., 1989).

Adults who are available and responsive to children are often those most able to communicate with children about emotions (Bretherton, 1990). Not surprisingly, preschool children with secure attachment organization histories do better than children with insecure attachment histories in tasks that assess emotional understanding—the ability to recognize and discuss emotions and their consequences (Laible & Thompson, 1998).

This association between adult's responsiveness and communication competence concerning emotions means that children with histories of insecure attachment organizations appear to have more dysfunctional patterns of communication about emotions. Children with insecure histories may defensively hide or distort anxious and angry feelings, appearing cool, apathetic, and expressionless in contexts where adults expect negative emotions (Kobak, 1999). These same "cool" children when exposed to extreme stress may engage in uncontrolled anger, fear, and sadness. Ethan in the following narrative may well be one of these children.

> Ethan has a very difficult time controlling himself. He is loud, insists on being the center of attention, and gets extremely angry when limits are set. Ethan is in a special education class for much of the school day, but is mainstreamed into a regular kindergarten for language arts. He had spent the previous hour in the special education classroom disrupting the entire class, falling repeatedly out of his chair onto the floor, talking in a silly voice, loudly demanding all the turns, and then throwing chairs, crying and yelling when he did not get more turns than the other children. His teacher's efforts to control him were fruitless.

Now Ethan has returned to his general education classroom.

> The children are all at different centers engaged in a variety of activities. During the first rotation Ethan is in a group with the teacher. He is still talking about how mad he is that he didn't get more turns. His teacher says, "I understand you were mad, but now it is time to read. Are you ready to join

us?" Ethan nods and takes his letter board. He decides he wants the one that makes a particular sound. The teacher says he can ask his friend if she will trade, and the trade is made. Ethan sits right next to the teacher. She uses a very soft voice and consistent demands to keep him from disrupting the work of the other students. She has to intervene with him repeatedly, but this is always done in a quiet voice and his behavior does not escalate.

Ethan's mainstream teacher is working to create a positive child-teacher relationship with Ethan. She keeps him in close proximity ("Ethan sits right next to the teacher"). She acknowledges his emotions ("I understand you were mad"), but focuses him on the task ("but now it is time to read. Are you ready to join us?"). She is proactive in helping him to avoid conflicts ("The teacher says he can ask his friend if she will trade and the trade is made").

When Ethan moves out of physical proximity to his teacher, he becomes disorganized. The teacher reestablishes contact with him and helps him regulate himself.

When Ethan's group rotates into the free choice area, he becomes immediately anxious and loud. He paces from one side of the room to the next, ignores the aides who are trying to intervene, and is unable to find something to do. He begins talking loudly to a friend. The teacher, who is now with another group of students, looks up and quietly admonishes him for disturbing their work. Ethan responds by saying in a very loud voice, "I didn't say you could listen to what I was saying. I am talking to my friend and you can't listen." Instead of responding verbally, she crooks her finger, inviting him over to her side. She quietly says, "If you weren't standing right in front of my group, talking in a very loud voice, then I wouldn't be able to hear what you are saying. You could go away from my group and speak softly to your friend." Ethan walks back to his friend, pulls him away from the group and whispers in his ear.

Ethan and his teacher are working to construct a mutually reciprocal relationship (Maccoby, 1984). In a mutually reciprocal relationship both partners work to negotiate mutually acceptable solutions to conflict. Early research examining links between mother-child attachment security and inhibitory control found that infants who were classified as secure were more compliant and showed less frustration and aggression as toddlers (Londerville & Main, 1981; Matas, Arend, & Sroufe, 1978). If children trust their adult attachment figure, then they are more willing and eager to be socialized (Kochanska, 1997). Furthermore, the experience of a mutually reciprocated relationship allows both partners, the child and the adult, to "feel invested in and responsible for each other's welfare; one feels concern for and acts responsively to the other's needs, and, at the same time, one comes to expect the other to be responsive to one's needs and to be concerned about one's welfare" (Kochanska, 1997, p. 94).

As we discussed in Chapter 1, attachment relationships can be constructed when children are preschoolers, of school age, or infants and with teachers as well as mothers. The idea of a mutually reciprocated relationship can be very useful in classrooms. If children and teachers and children and their peers all feel responsible for each other, then harmonious relationships and environments in which all children can learn are possible.

A mutually reciprocated relationship is very different from the adversarial relationship sometimes implied in the socialization and classroom-management literatures. In terms of behavioral interaction, when there is a mutually responsive relationship, there is a diminished need for adult use of power or coercion strategies. Because the child is eager to cooperate with the adult, socialization strategies do not need to be harsh or restrictive. In optimal situations, classrooms can be considered to consist of networks of mutually reciprocal child-teacher and child-child relationships embedded in a positive, prosocial environment.

Within this way of thinking, classroom management can be reconceptualized as processes that create positive child-teacher relationships. The construction of positive, prosocial classroom environments can be considered a substitute or a supplement for traditional classroom management. If a teacher constructs positive and secure attachment relationships with children such that there is a predominance of mutually reciprocated relationships, then classroom management becomes a matter of constructing, maintaining, and sustaining harmonious relationships, rather than of devising strategies for managing and avoiding potential conflict and disruption.

Adult Practices. In addition to looking at the role played by child-adult relationships in the development of internalized dispositions toward regulation and control, we need to consider adult practices. First we will review research linking adult practices with aggression and then linking adult practices with internalized disposition.

A relevant and well-regarded literature links harsh, punishing, and coercive parental discipline to children's aggressive and disruptive behaviors (cf. McFadyen-Ketchum, Bates, Dodge, & Pettit, 1996; Spieker, Larson, Lewis, Keller, & Gilchrist, 1999). Harsh and restrictive parental behaviors may be particularly significant influences for children with difficult life circumstances—those who have been abused and who have experienced family violence (Aber & Allen, 1987).

The definition of harsh and restrictive parental behaviors is often contextually dependent and difficult to interpret in terms of culturally appropriate behaviors. In our own research we find it important to simultaneously attend to context and to the emotional tone, behaviors, and affect of both participants, in order to interpret whether an interaction is harsh, restrictive, or firm or involves mutual teasing. This is an area of research where it is particularly important for the person assessing the interaction to be an insider in regard to culture, race, and class.

More recently, researchers have examined more proactive, prosocial parental practices that are associated with children's internalized regulation and control (Gottman, Katz, & Hooven, 1997). Adults who act as coaches for their children's expression and modulation of emotion and focus on social content are linked to children who are more successful at effortful control and emotional regulation. Adult emotional coaching includes responding to emotional displays, labeling the emotions, and in a supportive manner helping children with strategies to modulate their emotional displays. When adults coach children, the children are helped to develop their ability to inhibit negative affect, to self-sooth, and to focus their attention on the social context. That is, children are helped to cry or be otherwise upset without either losing control or acting aggressively.

In the narrative that follows, teacher Lillian uses emotional coaching when toddler Hector has an accident. She lets him know that it is OK to be sad when you fall.

> Hector, barely able to stand and walk, is trying to ride a toy car in an area of the playground covered with bark. He backs up and hits the curb. The car tips over backward. Bam! He hits the back of his head on the pavement. Lillian, his teacher, sees what happens and immediately moves toward him. Hector starts crying. Lillian squats down and scoops Hector into her arms. She says, "The car fell over, and you fell off. You hit your head, and it hurts." She continues talking softly with Hector until he stops sobbing and toddles off toward the water table.

In the following narrative, an older child, Amy, frequently tests limits and becomes oppositional and defiant when asked to comply with rules. A part of her teacher's work, as she moves to construct a more positive relationship between Amy and herself, is to help Amy name and understand her emotions.

> Amy runs onto the grassy area of the play yard. The grass is off limits because it has been newly planted. Amy is well aware of the restriction. Her teacher calls out to her, "Amy, we can't be on the grass today. Come on back up to the sand area." Amy moves farther away from the teacher, remaining on the grass. Her teacher follows her, "Amy, you need to come off

the grass. Can you do it by yourself, or do you need my help?" Amy continues to move away from the teacher, who follows her, takes her arm, and
escorts her from the grass. "That's not OK. You need to listen when I talk to
you." Amy begins to cry and protest loudly about wanting to be on the grass.
Her teacher says, "I know that makes you really mad when I stop you from
doing what you want to do, but we really can't be on the grass today. . . . it is
trying to grow." Amy continues to cry and protest. Her teacher sits with her,
validating her feelings, but maintaining the limit until she is calm enough to
play again.

Amy's teacher enforces her rule about where the children may play.
At the same time, she coaches Amy in naming and acknowledging angry
feelings.

In contrast to these examples of emotional coaching, some adults dis-
miss negative emotions and do not talk about them in a supportive manner.
When adults behave in this way, children have difficulty in regulating their
negative emotions and in focusing on the social and learning situation. An
example of this sequence of events occurs in the following narrative from a
kindergarten class.

Steven comes into the classroom after recess with a tear-streaked face. He
sits at his desk looking sad. Ms. Pointer is busy preparing material for a
project on *pan de muertos*. Steven stands up and walks over to the carpet.
He gets down on all fours and crawls under a table. He starts to bark loudly.
Jonah says, "Teacher, Steven isn't in his chair." Steven barks again.
Ms. Pointer says, "If we are going to make *pan de muertos*, everyone
needs to be in their chairs." Steven stays under the table. Jonah says again,
"Teacher." Ms. Pointer says, "Steven, please go back to your seat so the class
can make *pan de muertos*." Steven crawls out from under the table and
slowly walks to his seat. He lays his head down on the desk and does not
move. He begins to sob.

Ms. Pointer ignores the evidence of Steven's tears. He escalates his emotional display and misbehaves before Ms. Pointer attends to him. Eventually
his emotions are too overwhelming for him to participate in the classroom
learning activity, and he has disrupted the learning of the other children.

There is a growing body of empirical evidence to support the assumptions of Gottman and colleagues that emotional coaching is linked to internalized dispositions toward regulation and control. Children whose mothers
are observed to be more responsive to their children's emotional displays are
rated by independent observers as more socially and emotionally competent
(Denham & Holt, 1993). While this research included observations of all

types of emotional display, most studies focus on the negative emotions—distress, fear, and sadness. Some adults—parents and teachers—find it difficult to be responsive to children's display of negative emotion; instead, adults will ignore, minimize, or punish these displays. Empirical studies that observe parent and children's behavior find that this adult practice is linked to children who are less prosocial, more aggressive, and more avoidant of others (Carlson & Parke, 1996; Eisenberg et al., 1999; Eisenberg, Fabes, & Murphy, 1996).

In the following example, first grader Yasmine is distressed. Her teacher, Ms. Rosbos, appears to be more concerned about the testing procedures than in being responsive to Yasmine.

> Yasmine finishes her spelling test. With great enthusiasm she raises two hands, rather than one, to signal that she is done. Ms. Rosbos says, "If you are done raise just one hand." Ms. Rosbos then explains that the testing is not done and now they must pull out their math books. While trying to pull her math book from her desk, Yasmine drops her pencil and knocks a paper on the floor. She scrambles out of her chair to get the paper and pencil. Finally, she is sitting with her math book at her desk. Ms. Rosbos has asked the class to find test number 6. Yasmine, looking scared, fumbles with the pages of her math book. She begins to cry quietly. Ms. Rosbos says to the class, "If you are not ready you will have to make up time at recess."

In contrast, in the following narrative a teacher of a younger child responds to a child's negative emotion and helps the child reorient toward classroom activity. Ryan's dad has just left the child-care center after reading with his son. Two-year-old Ryan is fighting a cold and looks sad as the narrative begins. Patrice, Ryan's favorite teacher, is outside watching some toddlers play on the climbing structure.

> Ryan stands at the edge of the dramatic–play area. He absently pushes a small wheel toy against the railing as he watches Valda (another teacher) help Katie and Devon put on dresses. He yawns and rubs his eyes. Ryan looks up and spies teacher Patrice outside on the yard. He drops the toy and runs outside and hangs on to Patrice's arm. Patrice looks down, smiles, and says, "Are you feeling sad, Ryan?" Ryan says, "I want wubby."
>
> Patrice grabs Ryan's hand, leads him to his cubby and says, "Here is wubby." Ryan lets go of Patrice's hands and takes his blanket. He sticks the thumb of the hand holding the blanket into his mouth and follows Patrice. He puts his hand in a table filled with cornmeal. He takes a cup and fills it with cornmeal and says to Patrice, "Making cookies." Patrice replies, "What kind of cookies?" Ryan says, "Chocolate," and makes eating sounds: "Chomp, chomp."

We suspect that Patrice's attending to and labeling Ryan's emotional state provided the young child with tools for regulating his sadness and being able to turn to a learning experience within the classroom.

In summary, a rich and growing body of empirical research supports the preposition that children's relationships and interactions with adults influence children's internalized dispositions toward regulation and control. Children who have the experience of constructing a secure attachment relationship often also have the experience of an adult who helps them learn to regulate their emotions—by being responsive, accepting, and comforting. Children with secure attachment relationships tend to engage in a mutually reciprocated relationship within which conflicts can be resolved. Adults who engage in positive coaching concerning the expression of emotions, particularly negative emotions, are linked to children who are able to regulate and control their emotions.

LINKING CHILD-TEACHER RELATIONSHIPS TO HARMONIOUS INTERACTIONS

We turn now to a more limited body of empirical evidence for direct links between child-teacher relationships, children's internalized dispositions toward regulation and control, and harmonious interactions. Earlier research addressed this question indirectly by examining relations between security in child-teacher attachment and children's social competence with peers. In all these studies a part of the definition of social competence with peers included low levels of aggression. Children who were assessed as having more secure child-teacher attachments also were observed and rated to be more socially competent with peers (Howes, Hamilton, & Phillipsen, 1998; Raikes, 1993; van IJzendoorn et al., 1992). In these studies the quality of the mother-child relationship was statistically held constant, suggesting that the experience of constructing a secure child-teacher relationship was independently linked to social competence with peers.

Recently, a number of studies have more directly examined links between internalized dispositions and child-teacher relationships. Mitchell-Copeland, Denham, and DeMulder (1997) observed attachment security between preschool-age children and their teachers. Teachers rated children's social competence, peers rated likeability, and independent observers noted emotion regulation and how children reacted to the emotional displays of their peers within the preschool context. Children who were more secure with their teachers were more able to regulate their emotions, were more prosocial in response to peers, and were rated as more socially competent by their teachers.

Another longitudinal study examined changes in children's aggression with peers when children changed child-care teachers (Howes & Hamilton, 1993). In this study children were followed from their first birthdays when all were enrolled in child-care centers until they went to kindergarten. Every 6 months both aggression with peers and attachment security with teachers was observed. When children had a change in their primary child-care teacher and when the change was from an insecure relationship to a secure one, children decreased their aggression with peers.

This research provides evidence for similar processes linking child-teacher relationships to harmonious interactions, as did the research we just reviewed on parents. This is powerful evidence to support the notion that working to construct more trusting and secure child-teacher relationships can help children develop internalized dispositions toward regulation and control that in turn promote harmonious interactions in classrooms.

SUMMARY

We can conclude from the evidence presented in this chapter that creating harmonious interactions in classrooms involves much more than teachers presenting the rules for conduct. Instead, research suggests that we must consider the development and enhancement of children's internalized dispositions toward compliance and mutually reciprocated relationships if we wish to construct harmonious interactions within classrooms. Teachers who select this pathway generally believe that teaching and learning take place in a community of learners rather than through teacher-run lessons.

Our understanding of harmonious interactions in classrooms is derived from research inspired by developmental psychology and studies of parents rather than teachers. This research, collaborated by teacher behavior in classrooms, does suggest that with the construction of secure attachment relationships and emotional coaching by significant adults, children are predisposed toward harmonious rather than acrimonious interactions. Acrimonious interactions are linked in this same body of evidence to insecure attachment relationships and harsh and restrictive adult practices. This suggests that the commonsense advice handed down to novice teachers to be strict, to not smile, and to make children accountable for their misbehavior may all too often lead to harsh and restrictive classroom environments that are linked to more, rather than fewer, conflicts. In this context it is important to note that the most effective teachers we observed were able to preserve classroom rules of conduct that respected both individual and group learning while these teachers served as emotional coaches and worked to build positive attachment relationships.

3

Using Child-Teacher Relationships to Organize Classroom Learning and Climate

In the previous chapter we discussed how acrimonious interaction and con-flictual and nontrusting relationships with teachers can interfere with class-room learning. We now shift our attention to examine how positive teacher-child relationships can organize children's learning. Again, as in the previous two chapters, we rely on research for our evidence and use our narratives as illustrations.

Early childhood education includes schooling for children from birth to age 8. The educational goals for children in this age group include not only acquiring basic skills (most children learn to read and do basic mathematics during this developmental period), but also developing the capacity to learn (Katz & Chard, 1995). In this chapter we will argue that these educational attainments—basic skills and the capacity to learn—can be best achieved when children are in classrooms that foster exploration and independence or self-reliance. We also will argue that children are able to explore learning resources competently and self-reliantly when they have a positive relation-ship with their teacher and when the classroom provides a positive social and emotional environment.

EXAMINING EXPLORATORY COMPETENCE AND SELF-RELIANCE

Exploration is an important part of learning and developing the capac-ity to learn in early childhood. Classrooms, and the teachers who organize them, provide children with both opportunities and resources for learning. Within these classrooms children are commonly exposed to language arts experiences, including acting out stories and putting words to music; engaging in creative activities involving blocks, dramatic play, and art materials; and working with puzzles and other manipulatives designed to exercise fine-motor and spatial skills. It is commonly believed that through engaging in these learning and play activities children will acquire information and develop strategies for learning.

A second common assumption lies in the Vygotskian notion that more competent cognitive activities will occur when there is both a varied and rich environment and teachers who, through social interaction, enhance individual children's activities in this environment. Thus practitioners and researchers see cognitive activity as the product of an interaction between the classroom environment and the social interaction within that classroom.

Again, regardless of educational philosophy, a goal of schooling in the early childhood years is independent learning. Independence or self-reliance is another internal disposition—the child's motivation to explore, persistence in the face of frustration, and effective use of adults as resources. Independence or self-reliance plays a prominent role in a child's capacity to adapt to the challenges of school settings, including aspects of social interaction with peers, response to instruction, and motivation to perform academic tasks. Pianta (1998) argues that although independence appears to be a child-based skill or capacity, it too is deeply rooted within relationships. From this theoretical perspective, independence or self-reliance, like other internalized dispositions, is based both on the child's previous interactions and relationships and on the extent to which the classroom teacher provides a secure base for exploration.

In order to learn while exploring, children must be able to concentrate on exploring rather than being distracted. Attachment theory suggests that the ability to concentrate during exploration depends on

- The ability to organize emotions and behaviors to respond to novel events and materials open-mindedly and carefully.
- Confidence in the adult caregiver's availability and help, should help be needed (Grossman, Grossmann, & Zimmermann, 1999).

In this chapter we will continue our theme of linking relationships to internalized dispositions that enhance school success by focusing on exploration and self-reliance. The following narrative illustrates this linkage. We return to Ryan, the sad 2-year-old who was helped by his favorite teacher, Patrice, to regulate his negative emotions. In this narrative, Ryan is again playing in close proximity to Patrice.

> Patrice and Ryan are in the block area. Ryan begins by pulling all the blocks off the shelf. He then lines them up small end to small end in a trainlike formation. During this activity Patrice has been sitting close by, watching, but not interacting with Ryan. As Patrice watches, Ryan points to the blocks, looks at Patrice, and says, "I want to count. I want to count, I want to count." Patrice says, "What?" and leans closer to listen. Ryan says, "I want to count." Patrice points at the blocks and counts out loud, "1, 2, 3, 4, 5, 6." Ryan says the numbers after her and smiles.

In this narrative, Ryan was a competent explorer. He exploited the properties of the blocks, recognizing that they belonged to the same category, that they could be grouped according to similar characteristics, and that they could be counted. He appears not to be able to attach the number names to the blocks to be able to count, so he demonstrated self-reliance in asking for help when he needed it.

In the following narrative Sylvia and Charles, first graders, are both working at a literacy activity center. The activity center is really the side of a metal filing cabinet, so because of limited space, the children must move from sitting on the floor to standing to complete the task. Each child has a list of spelling words. Magnetic letters are stuck to the filing cabinet. The task is to make the spelling words with the magnet letters.

> Charles is searching for letters. He pushes all the letters down the cabinet toward the floor so that he has extra room for his words. He finds an *o* and an *f* and makes the word *of*. Charles looks at his list of words and then finds a *t* and an *o*, which he combines to make *to*. He finds the letters for *you* and *and*; after clearing more space, he makes those words. By now, all the leftover letters are jumbled near the bottom of the cabinet, and Sylvia has essentially no space to do the task. She is working on the word *and*. She takes the *a* from Charles's *and*. Charles says, "Stop taking my letters. I need the *a*." Sylvia calls for their teacher: "Ms. Hazen, help." Ms. Hazen asks, "How can we make this easier for both of you to work?" Sylvia suggests putting letters that are alike (the duplicates) together. Ms. Hazen agrees that that might work.

In this narrative, Charles was working independently but with no regard for the learning needs of the other social participant. Sylvia, in contrast to Charles, demonstrates self-reliance. When she cannot complete her work, she asks her teacher for help. She appears to trust that her teachers will help her solve the problem of being crowded out by Charles. With her teacher's support she can generate a suggestion that solves the problem.

LINKING ATTACHMENT TO EXPLORATION
AND SELF-RELIANCE

The construct of exploration is an essential part of attachment theory. Children who have secure attachment organizations are competent explorers; they believe that they can explore and that they are worthy of help (Bowlby, 1982; Grossman et al., 1999). Children who have avoidant attachment organizations may be able to focus on exploring in order to avoid the attachment figure, but their anxiety about the attachment figure restricts their ability to concentrate and to ask for help when needed. Children who have resistant attachment organizations are restricted in their exploration because of their preoccupation with the whereabouts and activities of the attachment figure. The following narrative provides an interesting contrast between Wendy, who demonstrates self-reliance, and Joseph, whose insecure attachment relationship with the teacher is linked to his inability to explore and benefit from a learning activity.

> Several children decide that they would like to dance during free-choice time. The teacher puts on music in one corner of the room and then returns to engage with other children in the house area. The children dance happily. They set up chairs for musical chairs; they march around the tables. The tape ends.
>
> Wendy goes to the house area and asks the teacher to change the tape. The teacher does so and the children return to their dancing. Wendy suggests to the other children that they use instruments, and she runs over to the house area to ask her teacher for the instruments. Once again the dancing resumes. The other children continue to dance, and Wendy walks back over to the house area. The teacher asks her if she is through dancing. She says, "No. I just came to say hi." The teacher gives her a hug, and Wendy returns to the music area.
>
> Another child, Joseph, has been engaged in the same dancing activity. During the dancing, dozens of times, he has stopped dancing, stood still, and said in a low voice that he would like to listen to a particular song. However, he has remained on the opposite side of the room from the teacher, and she cannot hear him. When the teacher approaches the group, he turns his back on her, and the song is never played.

Because Wendy and Joseph are part of the Children with Difficult Life Circumstance Study, we assessed their child-teacher attachment relationships. Wendy and her teacher have constructed a secure relationship, whereas Joseph and the teacher have an avoidant relationship. Wendy is able to ask for help and "check in" with her teacher, using her as a secure base for exploration. Joseph appears to want help from the teacher, but he does not approach her or ask for assistance. The teacher is occupied with other children and misses Joseph's signals. Wendy's signals are clear and positive. She makes it easy for the teacher to give her support while continuing to work with other children.

These assumed relationships between attachment organization, exploration of a learning involvement, and independence or self-reliance have been most completely tested through assessing mother-child attachment. Infants with secure child-mother attachment organizations (when compared with infants with insecure attachment organizations) spent longer time concentrating when they played with novel toys (Main, 1983), and paid more attention to the environment (Belsky, Garduque, & Hrnic, 1984). Toddlers with secure as opposed to insecure child-mother attachments showed more enthusiasm and delight in play, were more deeply engrossed in their activities, showed greater versatility in exploring different aspects of toys, and were more effective in their efforts to master challenging tasks (Main, 1983; Matas et al., 1978). Preschool children who were assessed as having had secure maternal attachment organizations as infants were more persistent in a laboratory task and engaged in more concentrated play (Grossman et al., 1999; Suess, Grossmann, & Sroufe, 1992).

A second longitudinal study found a relationship between early mother-child attachment organization and later independence or self-reliance (Sroufe, 1983). The focus of this study was dependency—the inverse of independence and self-reliance; dependent children were defined as those who inappropriately seek attention from teachers and are extremely reliant on them for help. Children with early secure maternal attachment organizational histories did ask their preschool teachers for help, but in positive ways and at times when the teachers judged that they genuinely needed help. Children with insecure maternal attachment organizational histories were judged to be more dependent as preschoolers (Sroufe, 1983), as 10-year-olds (Urban, Carlson, Egeland, & Sroufe, 1991), and as 15-year-olds (Sroufe, Carlson, & Shulman, 1993).

Given our assumption that success in school depends not only on learning basic skills, but also on internalized dispositions toward learning—competent exploration and self-reliance—we would expect that children who have early secure maternal attachment organizations would be successful in school. A number of studies support this assumption (Cohn, 1990; Pianta & Harbers, 1996).

LINKING CHILD-TEACHER ATTACHMENT ORGANIZATION AND LEARNING IN SCHOOL

As we have argued throughout this book, other adults, including teachers, can function in a manner similar to that of mothers in the development of internalized dispositions and interaction patterns. This theoretical assumption and findings from an early study of kindergarten children at risk for school failure (Alexander, Entwistle, & Thompson, 1987) have focused attention on child-teacher relationships in early childhood education.

Recall that early childhood covers a wide developmental period (birth to age 8) and includes many different schooling contexts—infant and toddler child care, preschool, and early elementary school. When children are infants and toddlers, their child-care caregivers, often called teachers, perform many of the same caregiving tasks as parents, and in the parents' absence the child must depend on the teacher for survival and social needs. When children are older, in preschool and elementary school, teachers perform fewer caregiving tasks, but still function as attachment figures, especially as children use teachers to organize their activities, particularly their exploration of the learning environment. Therefore, we assume that children who have more secure child-teacher-attachment organizations will be better able to succeed in school.

In the following narrative, collected in a kindergarten class, James is using his teacher, Ms. Kaya, to organize his attempts to match sounds, letters, and pictures. James and two other children are sitting with Ms. Kaya at a small table. On the table are pictures of animals. Ms. Kaya hands each child a card with a letter on it; the task is to find a picture of an animal that begins with that letter.

> James has an *h*. He leans forward to the center of the table and pulls out a picture of a horse. Smiling up at Ms. Kaya, he says, "I have a hunting horse." He makes the picture move in a galloping action. Ms. Kaya says, "What letter do you have?" He looks up at her with a confused look on his face and does not answer. Christal, who has been watching, says, "*H*." Ms. Kaya asks James, "What animal do you have?" James says, "Hunting horse," and sings the horse sound, part of the zoo song. Ms. Kaya says, "Yes, an *h* for a horse."
>
> Ms. Kaya hands out new letters. James says, "I've got a *g*." He shuffles through the animal cards. "I can't find mine, I need a *g*." Jesse looks at him and says, "*G* right here." James says to Ms. Kaya, "I've got Gordo Gorilla."

We can infer that James trusts Ms. Kaya. He does not avoid her (as does Joseph in the previous narrative) or engage in conflict with Jesse (e.g., "She took my gorilla"), which would focus attention on him but interfere with his learning.

There is a growing body of research to support the assumptions that children who have more secure child-teacher-attachment organizations will be better able to succeed in school. One observation study using a large sample includes both the infant-toddler and preschool developmental periods (Howes

& Smith, 1995b). In this study, 840 children enrolled in full-time center-based child care were observed. Children ranged in age from 10 to 70 months. The study tested the prediction that variation in children's cognitive activities could be explained by child-care quality, teacher behavior, children's activities, and observed attachment security with child-care teachers. For all ages, and for all ethnic groups, children who had secure attachment organizations with their teachers were most engaged in competent exploration of the environment and in enhanced cognitive activity. What appeared to be important was the child's felt security with the teacher rather than particular behaviors with her or him.

A second longitudinal study provides evidence for some continuity in the relationship between children's child-teacher attachment organizations and school learning (Howes, Hamilton, & Phillipsen, 1998). Children's attachment organization with their first child-care teacher was observed as was their mother-child attachment organization at 12 months of age. When the children were 9 years old, we asked them to tell us stories about their current teachers. We used these stories to rate their current trusting relationship with their teacher. Children who were more trusting of their teachers were the same children who had had positive relationships with their first child-care teacher, not the children who had secure child-mother relationships. This suggests that children's early initial experiences with teachers may serve to organize their school behaviors and their relationships with their elementary school teachers.

Other studies linking competent exploration with child-teacher attachment organization have tended to use teacher reports rather than observations of child-teacher attachment organization. As we discussed in Chapter 1, teachers and observers tend to agree about the quality of child-teacher relationships. In a longitudinal study that followed the same children from preschool to kindergarten, we found that teacher perceptions of the quality of child-teacher relationship tended to be consistent within preschool and across the preschool to kindergarten transition (Howes, Phillipsen, & Peisner-Feinberg, 2000). This suggests that the children entered formal school with a working model of child-teacher relationships and with established patterns of engaging teachers. Despite differing role definitions of preschool versus kindergarten teachers, children and kindergarten teachers tend to construct relationships consistent in quality with that of preschool child-teacher relationships.

The children in this last study were part of the Cost, Quality, and Outcomes (CQO) study, a longitudinal study of children enrolled in center-based child care as preschoolers and followed into second grade. The primary focus of the CQO study was academic achievement. In the CQO study, child-teacher-relationship quality in preschool predicted both the quality of the child-teacher relationship and academic and social success in elementary school (Peisner-Feinberg et al., 2001). Similar connections between child-teacher-relationship quality and academic success are found across the kindergarten year (Birch & Ladd, 1997); from kindergarten into first grade (Pianta, Steinberg, & Rollins, 1997); and from kindergarten through eighth grade (Hamre & Pianta, 2002).

INTERACTING WITH PEERS AND LEARNING IN SCHOOL

When considering the classroom learning environment, we need to include the children's classmates. Not only do children's experiences with peers contribute to the growth of their social skills—their capacity to develop personal relationships and to cooperate, negotiate, and resolve conflicts. In addition, work in cooperative groups is an important source of basic skills learning within early childhood classrooms. The internalized dispositions toward competent and self-reliant exploration are particularly important when children work in groups. Learning can be disrupted by acrimonious interaction, as well as when members of a cooperative learning group are distracted or are dependent.

In the following narrative, learning is disrupted by the acrimonious behavior of one of the kindergarten children. Andre, Maria, and Shasha have been assigned to work at the block table. Their learning goal is to decide how many red, green, and blue blocks will be needed to replicate the geometric design placed on the table before them. The unit blocks are much larger and heavier than the blocks depicted on the design sheet.

Maria and Shasha decide to make the unit blocks look just like the blocks on the paper. Then they will count the blocks of each color and find the answer. They work seriously and intently. Occasionally, one or the other of them will suggest another strategy. They look back to the design sheet and then at the emerging block structure.

Andre has taken no part in the preliminary discussions or in the building of the design sheet replica. Suddenly, in a very angry tone, Andre says, "What are you doing? Just tell me what you are doing? What are you doing?" Maria stops working and looks up at him. She points to the design sheet and says, "We are making it look like that." Andre interrupts, "I'm not talking to you. I'm talking to her."

He points at Shasha. He gets a block and holds it over Shasha's head. "Tell me what you are doing and I won't hurt you with this block." Shasha stops working and looks frightened. Maria says, "We are working on this." Andre says, "Do it this way." Shasha leaves the table and hovers next to her teacher on the other side of the room. Her teacher looks up and in an annoyed voice says, "Shasha, what are you doing here? Why aren't you doing your work?"

Andre's acrimonious behavior disrupted the competent and self-reliant *and* collaborative exploration of Maria and Shasha. Maria attempts to resolve the problem, and Shasha, who was physically threatened, seeks help. It is virtually impossible for a teacher to observe everything that goes on in a busy classroom. It is therefore important for teachers to remember to ask questions about what is happening, rather than making assumptions and sometimes drawing incorrect conclusions. In this case, the teacher did ask Shasha what she was doing, but the tone suggested that she was annoyed and did not really invite the child into dialogue or explanation.

Learning also can be disrupted when children are distracted. In the next narrative, second grader Moise wants to win the prize for the group that first achieves the answer. His focus on winning means that Maritza has no chance to participate in the learning activity.

Ms. Martinez assigns the children to three–person groups and tells them that the first group to correctly write the definitions for the vocabulary list will get 10 minutes of extra recess.

Moise, Maritza, and Jesus are in one group. All three children speak Spanish at home. Maritza has almost no English. Moise and Jesus are fluent in English as well as Spanish.

The vocabulary task is all in English. Moise says, "OK, she can't help because she doesn't know English. Jesus, you write, and I'll look up the words. That way will be fastest."

The two boys work diligently. Maritza initially is looking at the dictionary with Moise, but soon sits quietly, eyes down. Ms. Martinez appears not to notice the group dynamics.

When Moise puts up his hand and says, "We finished." Ms. Martinez joins the group, corrects the vocabulary list, and excuses them to go to recess.

We can only speculate about the child-teacher relationships of the children in this group. From our observations, we worry that Maritza will feel that she can not trust Ms. Martinez or the other children to help her feel part of the group. Certainly she has learned no vocabulary words as a result of this exercise. With repeated experiences similar to this one, Maritza may become more and more disengaged from school.

In the following narrative we see how second grader Monica's behavior, consistent with an insecure dependent relationship with Ms. Maya, interferes with her learning and the learning of the group.

Monica and Kennedy are to work together to complete a worksheet based on their last reading assignment. Kennedy organizes the task and says, "The first question is . . . ; let's go back and read the first part to make sure."

Monica interrupts, "Let's ask Ms. Shima for help. I don't understand." Monica puts up her hand, waves it around and looks for her teacher.

The teacher is working with other children. When she does not immediately respond, Monica leaves Kennedy and goes over to tug on the teacher's arm.

Monica cannot focus on the learning task when she is preoccupied with the child-teacher relationship. Her anxiety and lack of self-reliance interrupt Kennedy's learning as well as her own.

These three narratives illustrate our premise that learning in cooperative groups cannot take place when children lack the social skills to collaborate with peers or are preoccupied with a problematic child-teacher relationship. In the first narrative, one child's acrimonious behavior disrupted the competent behavior of the group. In the second narrative, one child's clever analysis of how to win the prize interfered with the learning of another. In the third narrative, one child's troubled relationship with the teacher disrupted the entire group.

THE ROLE OF THE TEACHER:
PROVIDING A SECURE BASE FOR CHILDREN
TO EXPLORE THE WORLD OF PEERS

Young children need to be competent explorers of the world of peers as well as the learning environment. They also use teachers as secure (or not secure) bases for exploring this world (Howes, 1999; Pianta, 1998). We expect that children who construct secure attachment relationships with their teacher will use that adult as a base and a resource for entering the peer group. In the mother-child-attachment literature, there is ample evidence that children who have secure mother-child attachment relationships engage in more positive peer interactions than children with insecure mother-child attachment relationships (Cohn, 1990; Sroufe, 1983).

These findings suggest that, indeed, children with secure maternal attachment relationships use their mothers as a base to explore the world of peer interactions and relationships. As we discussed in the previous chapter, similar connections have been found for child-teacher attachment organizations. Children who have secure child-teacher attachment organizations are more competent with peers (Howes, 1999; Raikes, 1993; van IJzendoorn et al., 1992). These correlations between secure attachment and social competence with peers are particularly significant when children are young and newly exposed to peers. A secure relationship with an attachment figure facilitates the beginning development of social interaction with peers.

In the following narrative we revisit Jenn and Maricel, both 14-month-old toddlers, who are simultaneously figuring out how to use a slide with a four-step ladder and to engage with peers. Sylvia, their teacher, serves as a secure base in this process.

> Jenn and Maricel get stuck on the slide and both children turn to look at teacher Sylvia, who is sitting next to the slide. The children start on the slide again.
>
> Sylvia says, "Jenn, if you wait to let go until no one is on the slide you will not run into Maricel."
>
> Jenn again climbs the ladder and hovers on the top of the slide. The slide is clear, and she starts down. When she is still partway down, Maricel climbs up the ladder and slides down immediately, and the two children create another traffic jam on the slide.
>
> Again both children look at Sylvia, who laughs, gets up, and gently untangles them. She gives both children a hug and says, "Let's try this again. One at a time. Maricel, watch for Jenn. Jenn, watch for Maricel."
>
> This time both Maricel and Jenn wait at the top until the slide is clear. When Jenn is at the bottom of the slide and Maricel at the top, they look at each other and giggle. When the positions are reversed, Jenn at the top and Maricel at the bottom, they again peek and giggle. Sylvia smiles and laughs with them and remains sitting near the side.

In this narrative Sylvia remains in touch, physically and emotionally, with the children. Through her calm, positive tone, she helps the children understand how the slide works and encourages them to attend to each other. Another teacher strategy could have been to enforce a rule, "Only one on the slide," or to reprimand Jenn for "hurting Maricel and not watching what she was doing." Instead, Sylvia recognizes that the children are experimenting with a new and unfamiliar experience, each coordinating actions with another novice in playing games with peers. She is available, responsive, and willing to let the children solve this problem with just the right amount of help from her.

Older children, particularly in elementary school, enter classrooms with relationship histories, not only with adults but also with peers. Children with secure adult-child attachment organizational histories would as younger children have perceived peers as potentially fun and interesting social partners, entered into peer play, and with experience become socially skilled. Children with insecure adult-child attachment relationship histories as younger children have had less successful peer interactions and would have perceived peers as hostile or threatening and thus would have withdrawn from or exhibited aggression toward peers.

Once a child has withdrawn from peers or has constructed antagonistic patterns of interaction and relationships, it may be especially difficult for him or her to develop alternative behaviors with peers. Children quickly earn a reputation with peers, and unlike some sensitive adults who can understand that what appear to be hostile behaviors are based on mistrust, peers may perceive the potential peer partner as unpleasant and to be avoided. A skillful adult can work to disconfirm a child's hostile or withdrawing behavior, but a peer is more likely to react in ways that maintain the hostile relationship. Once the negative patterns of engaging with peers are established, they are resistant to change (Coie, 1990).

Recent research suggests that children who begin kindergarten being either aggressive with peers or aggressive and withdrawn from peers tend to continue to have difficulties with peers and develop conflictual relationships with teachers from kindergarten through second grade (Ladd & Burgess, 1999). The children who were seen by others as aggressive or aggressive and withdrawn reported that they were lonely, were dissatisfied with their social contacts, had few friends, and were the victims themselves of peer aggression. Children who perceive their social world as unfriendly have difficulties in using the peer group as a support for learning in school. Children who are preoccupied with poor peer relations are unlikely to have the skills or the internalized dispositions toward learning to be able to effectively interact in cooperative learning situations. In our next narrative, Malcolm is a child who fits this description.

Malcolm, age 6, is a bright boy, but he is loud and pushy and likes to be in charge of everything. He has a particularly hard time during cooperative group activities. His difficulties were so extreme that for the first part of the school year, he simply worked alone. Ms. Gomez has noticed that Malcolm has few friends, and she has decided to reintroduce him into cooperative groups.

> Students are working on large sheets of paper. Their task is to draw an imaginary automobile and then supply as many adjectives as possible to describe the car. Malcolm's group is small, only four students, instead of the usual six. One of the students, Tia, begins to draw. Malcolm snatches the marker from her hand, saying, "Let me do it, I can do it better."
>
> Anticipating trouble, Ms. Gomez was nearby. She sits down with the group and says, "This group is small, may I join in?"
>
> The students agree, and she remains to help negotiate the problems and to participate in the group. With her by his side, Malcolm is able to let Tia draw.

With support from his teacher, Malcolm is able to engage in behaviors that may make him more acceptable to his peers as a learning partner. We hope that with repeated experiences like this, Malcolm will be able to work with peers on his own. Perhaps his classmates will appreciate his ideas and be more willing to include him.

Newly constructed, more positive teacher-child relationships can help move children with prior negative peer relationships toward more positive peer interactions. In the following narrative, a child who has severe problems with peer relations is able to modulate his more negative behaviors with peers because he uses his increasingly positive relationship with his teacher as an organizer.

Roland, age 7, has a great deal of difficulty in school. He is really in need of a special day class but the process of obtaining appropriate services is slow and he remains in a regular second-grade classroom. He has daily problems with aggression and poor impulse control. It is January, and he continues to throw things, tackle students in the middle of the room, and entertain his classmates by eating crayons and attaching paperclips to his ears. Efforts at suspensions, behavior charts, and special privileges have had no effect.

His teacher, Ms. Sharp, spends a great deal of time and energy on Roland. She has made a home visit, eats lunch with him often, and gives him after-school jobs in the classroom, during which time they chat. She admires his artwork and works to be sensitive in her responses to his very disruptive behavior. In the following narrative Roland uses his emerging positive relationship with Ms. Sharp to modulate his behavior with peers.

> It is 8:30 a.m. and Roland has just arrived at school. He stayed late the previous day and helped Ms. Sharp set up the new computers in the classroom. He says to Ms. Sharp as he arrives, "Remember how I helped you yesterday?" Ms. Sharp replies, "I could not have done it without you, Roland. Thank you so much!"
>
> As the class begins, Ms. Sharp publicly praises Roland and lets all the students know of his hard work in setting up the computers. The students are excused one table at a time to get dictionaries. Roland leaps from his seat and starts to shove his classmates aside. He glances at Ms. Sharp, who shakes her head at him. He slows down, picks up a dictionary, and returns to his seat. He glances up again and finds Ms. Sharp smiling at him.

Roland, much older and with a complex relationship history, used the same behavior organization with his teacher as did Jenn and Maricel, who used their positive relationships with their teacher to organize their exploration of the world of peers.

SUMMARY

We take the influence of positive child-teacher relationships one step further in this chapter. In the previous chapter we presented evidence to argue that positive child-teacher relationships were linked to harmonious interactions within classrooms. When there are harmonious interactions instead of conflictual ones, learning can take place. In this chapter we have presented evidence to argue that children use their child-teacher relationships to organize their learning. We suggest that learning takes place when children engage in competent and self-reliant exploration, using classroom materials and their teacher as resources to extend their knowledge. We argue that children who are insecure and dependent on their teacher cannot competently explore their environment, because their child-teacher relationships interfere with their self-reliance. Likewise, we argue that children who are insecure and avoidant with their teacher cannot competently explore what is around them because they are preoccupied with avoiding the teachers. In these children, false independence interferes with their self-reliance.

We further extend these ideas by including peers as learning resources or inhibitors. We suggest that young children use their child-teacher attachment organization as a secure base for learning how to engage with peers and how to share the physical resources of the classroom. Through the efforts of caring teachers who work with the children to construct secure child-teacher attachment relationships, even older children with a history of problematic peer relationships can begin to competently explore the world of peers.

Teacher Behaviors and Classroom Organizations that Foster Trusting Child-Teacher Relationships

Part II shifts from a focus on describing child–teacher attachment relationship organizations, harmonious interactions, and classroom learning environments to an analysis of teacher practices resulting in both positive and less positive child-teacher relationships and classroom climates. We draw from our observations of more and less successful teachers and classroom climates to illustrate the strategies that these teachers employed. It is important to note that we do not believe that these strategies could or should be transported into other class-rooms and used by other teachers without careful attention to the individual needs of children and considerable reflection by teachers.

We have shifted our evidentiary base as we move from Part I to Part II. Recall that in Part I we used published research as evidence for our claims and used our narrative study to provide illustrations of the research findings. In Part II we use both published research and the narrative studies presented in this book as evidence to support our conclusions. In selecting narratives to include in Part II, we primarily used those that either represented the trends in the narrative data or represented an outlying or alternative viewpoint. Recall that in two of our three narrative studies—Children from Difficult Life Circumstances and Best Practices—we preselected classrooms that served children from difficult life circumstances in a reflective manner. Our analysis of these narratives helped us understand and describe the classroom practices we report as resulting in positive child–teacher relationships and classroom climates. The narratives from the Classroom Observation Study were not from classrooms preselected on the basis of their promoting positive relationships or climates. When we analyzed these narratives, we were interested in replicating examples of the positive practices that we identified in the other two studies and in understanding counterexamples of practices that appeared to result in conflictual relationships and acrimonious climates.

In Chapter 4 we review evidentiary support for the assumption that teachers can disconfirm children's patterns of interaction as they work with them to co-construct more positive child–adult relationships. In order to do this, we review the research on relationship formation and practices used in programs that engendered positive relationships in children from difficult life circumstances. We suggest that school can be different from home, particularly for children who do not have positive relationships within their homes. We acknowledge that teachers need support in the form of mentoring and reflective supervision as they work to change children's representations and behaviors concerning relationships.

In Chapter 5 we focus on specific teacher behaviors that foster more trusting child–teacher relationships within the classroom. We draw on research linking adult patterns of interaction to secure child–caregiver attachment rela-tionships, and we examine our narrative records within classrooms and relate them to practices within positive classroom contexts. We pay particular attention to developmental transitions in adult behaviors—noting that an exemplar of responsive behavior in a toddler classroom will be different from an exemplar in a second-grade classroom.

In Chapter 6 we continue this theme of adult facilitation of positive relation-ships with an emphasis on classroom organization rather than on specific teacher behaviors. We examine the research on classroom organization for implications for child–teacher relationships. We again use our narrative data to examine associations between strategies of classroom organization, harmonious child–teacher interaction, and positive child–teacher relationships. We identify several categories of classroom organization that emerged from these explorations: routines, cooperative learning, and teacher continuity. We explore the implica-tions of these classroom organizations for positive classroom climate.

4

Teachers and Children's Prior Relationship History: What Can Change?

Among professional educators, one can hear expressions of very contra-
dictory points of view: "It's all the parents' fault. How can we even begin
to teach these children when their home lives are so disruptive, angry,
distrustful?" and "Successful adults who were resilient children look back
and attribute their own overcoming the odds to a teacher who believed in
them."

In this chapter we will argue that teachers can make a difference, that
they can change children's patterns of relationships. This can happen only
when teachers are willing to attend to the influences of children's past relationship history and to act in ways that disconfirm negative behaviors associated with that history.

We begin the chapter with a description of how prior relationship history
influences current child-teacher interaction. We then discuss why what happens at home does not have to happen at school. In order to begin to understand how school can be different from home, we describe developmental
processes in relationship formation. We end this chapter by discussing research
on interventions to change the quality of child-teacher relationships. The content of these interventions form the framework for the remaining chapters in
this part on teacher behaviors and classroom organizations that foster trusting child-teacher relationships.

THE INFLUENCE OF PRIOR RELATIONSHIP HISTORY

Children come to school with an attachment organization that functions
as a working model of adult-child relationships (Bowlby, 1982). Children
use their working model as a map or blueprint for ways in which to engage
with new caregiving adults, and when children encounter a new adult, such
as a teacher, they tend to act toward her or him in ways that are consistent

with their prior relationship history, their working model. This behavior may have been successful in the past, but, particularly in the school environment, will not lead to a positive relationship (Sroufe, 1983). For example, children with maladaptive prior attachment histories may "set the teacher up" for replicating distrustful insecure relationships. In the following narrative we illustrate how a well-meaning teacher gets drawn into a prolonged and tedious exchange with a child who brings to the classroom a working model of an ambivalent/resistant attachment organization.

In our home observations, Ben, a preschooler, was classified as ambivalent/resistant with his mother. In the narrative, he engages with Ms. Garcia, an inexperienced teacher's aide, using patterns of interaction that were probably adaptive in his mother-child relationship, but in a school setting interfere with his and the other children's learning. As the narrative illustrates, the well-intended Ms. Garcia gets pulled into a prolonged engagement with Ben that not only does not provide him with opportunities for learning, but totally removes both of them from the classroom activities. The narrative takes place during free play. Perhaps in an effort to engage in positive interaction with Ben, Ms. Garcia approaches him with a feathered fan.

> She touches his face with the fan and says, "It is soft, like a bird." Ben turns from Ms. Garcia and hits one dinosaur with another and then laughs.
> Ms. Garcia responds to Ben with, "It's not funny. I'm not going to laugh."

There is a school rule that prohibits hitting dolls and replica animals as well as "real" people. As we will see in another narrative from this school, the rule is intended (and in some of our observations appears to work) to help children feel safe in school. The children in this school have all been homeless. Many of them have witnessed or experienced family or neighborhood violence. When the no-hitting rule is evoked with an explanation of the reason for the rule, some of the children we observed appeared to be comforted. In this particular narrative, Ms. Garcia does not provide an explanation for the rule. Instead she responds to Ben's provocative action by dismissing his emotional display (laughing) as inappropriate. Ben immediately escalates the interaction.

> He pushes a dinosaur so that it falls off a shelf and hits Sara on the head. Sara cries. Ms. Garcia walks to Sara and says, "Sorry, Sara. That hit you right on the head." Sara touches her head. Ms. Garcia strokes Sara's head and says, "Oh, that must have hurt." Ben peers around the corner, laughing. Ms. Garcia frowns and says, "It's not funny." She leaves Sara, picks up a doll, and hands it to Ben. Ben hits the doll and walks away.

By handing Ben a doll without explanation, Ms. Garcia almost invites him to engage in more forbidden hitting activity. Again she dismisses his emotions and provides no explanation for the no-hitting rule. Ben's behavior is illustrative of that of the children discussed in Chapter 2 who defensively hide or distort anxious and angry feelings, appearing cool (Kobak, 1999). As the episode continues, Ben loses all control of his actions and emotions.

> Ms. Garcia picks Ben up and says, "You don't hit things." Ben hits Ms. Garcia. She holds him and says, "I'm not going to let you down. It seems to me that you have decided that you are not going to play nice, that you need help." Ben cries, squirms his body, and pulls Ms. Garcia's hair. Ms. Garcia says, "I'm going to put you on the floor."
>
> Before she can put him down, Ben cries loudly. Ms. Garcia pulls him back up on her lap. She says, "You need to cry a little. Yes. I'll take care of you, dear, Yes, Yes." Ben cries very loudly and shouts (muffled by sobs), "I want down." Ms. Garcia replies, "I can't understand you." Ben repeats, shouting and sobbing, "I want down." Ms. Garcia replies, "You want down, OK, I'll let you down. I know."
>
> She remains standing, holding Ben, and rocking him in her arms. This sequence of Ben asking to be put down and Ms. Garcia holding him continues for 6 more minutes until Ms. Garcia removes Ben from the room. She walks out, still carrying him. He is sobbing out of control.

Both Ms. Garcia and Ben lost out on an opportunity to negotiate another type of relationship. We also suspect that both Ben and Ms. Garcia were left distressed. We can imagine that Ben does not feel that school is a safe place where the teachers will take care of him. He was likely confused by the inconsistencies between Ms. Garcia's words and her actions. We can imagine that Ms. Garcia is upset and may feel hopeless and without resources to work with children who are difficult. Interacting with children who enter school with insecure attachment organizations requires teachers to be particularly reflective and self-conscious if they are to develop positive relationships. In the section that follows we review the research evidence that supports the notion that teachers can disconfirm children's prior relationships. Then we explore through narrative analysis how the teachers we worked with created alternative child-teacher relationships.

RESEARCH ON DIFFERING CHILD-ADULT RELATIONSHIPS

Most of the evidence that suggests that teachers can be successful in constructing relationships that are different from children's prior child-adult relationships comes from studies of typical children in child-care settings (Goossen & van IJzendoorn, 1990; Howes, 1999; Mitchell-Copeland et al., 1997; van IJzendoorn et al., 1992). In all these studies, the researchers made independent assessments of the quality of mother-child-attachment relationships and the quality of the child-teacher relationship when the children had had at least several months of being cared for in the child-care setting. Children in these studies constructed different qualities of relationships with their child-care teachers from those they had with their mothers. The quality of the children's child-teacher relationships could be explained through observing teacher behaviors with the children. Teachers engaged more positively with children who were securely attached to them and less positively with children who were insecurely attached to them (Howes & Smith, 1995a). As we reviewed in preceding chapters, children who were more securely attached to their teachers were also more socially competent and less prone to behavior problems (Howes & Ritchie, 1999; Mitchell-Copeland et al., 1997).

Certainly there are children with difficult life circumstances included in the child-care samples, but these children were not examined separately from their more fortunate peers. However, there are a few studies that examine the child-teacher relationships of children with difficult life circumstances. Longitudinal studies of high-risk, but resilient, children find that the social networks of these children include at least one teacher who provided emotional support (Anthony & Cohler, 1987; Rutter, Maughan, Mortimore, & Ousten, 1979; Werner, 1993). The idea that child-teacher relationships need not replicate maladaptive mother-child relationships can empower a teacher in a situation in which she or he may feel hopeless. Relationships that are more positive than those that children have previously experienced can provide children with the opportunity not only to interact with a consistent and trustworthy adult, but also to view themselves as valuable human beings, worthy and deserving of attention and affection.

Other relevant research is on abused and neglected children. These children are likely to have insecure attachment relationships with their parents. But after 2 months in high-quality shelter care almost half of the toddlers removed from homes because of maternal abuse or neglect had developed a secure relationship with a caregiver (as assessed with the AQS) (Howes & Segal, 1993). Children who had remained in the shelter longer were more secure than children with shorter stays. As with more typical children, these children were most likely to form secure attachment relationships with caregivers who were rated as more sensitive.

In another study, we observed the attachment organization at home and at school of 22 preschool children removed from regular schools because of behavior problems and enrolled in a therapeutic school. Only three children (14%) were secure in their home attachment relationship; two of these three children were also secure at school. Within 2–6 months after enrollment in the therapeutic school, 26% of the children with insecure home attachment organizations had constructed an attachment organization at school that was more secure than their home attachment organization. These findings support the idea that home attachment organizations do not have to be replicated at school. However, as we have said, constructing positive and trusting child-teacher relationships when the child comes to school with a maladaptive working model is not an easy task. In the remaining sections of this chapter we discuss processes that can foster the construction of trusting, secure child-teacher relationships.

THE DEVELOPMENT OF CHILD-TEACHER RELATIONSHIPS

Child-teacher relationships take time to develop. First the child and teacher need to form a relationship. After the relationship is formed, it must be maintained. We found that teachers who worked to form positive relationships moved from relationship organizers to relationship partners.

Forming a Relationship

How do teachers and children construct attachment relationships? A mother and child begin to construct an attachment relationship from the moment of the child's birth, and attachment relationships develop simultaneously with children's repertoires of social interactive behaviors and their capacity for cognitive representation. Most children develop their child-teacher relationships after they have developed patterns of interaction and already have internal representations of relationships. With our colleagues we have conducted two studies that examine the processes of relationship formation. One study was conducted with toddler-age children in their first 6 months in a university child-care center (Howes & Oldham, 2001). Most of these children entered child care "ready" to construct positive attachment relationships. They directed attachment behaviors toward the caregivers, acting as if they expected caregivers to take care of them. To the extent that caregivers played their part and sensitively engaged the children in positive social interaction, these expectations were fulfilled.

We watched a child much like the others in this study on the first day in a child-care center for children of teen mothers.

> Gabriella is moving back and forth in the sandbox. She moves one step forward then one step back, then wiggles her shoulders and head. No teacher engages with her; they are all doing something with other children.

Maria, the teacher assigned to Gabriella's class, moves to the bench in the paved area to put on Yasmine's shoes. Gabriella stands still and watches Maria. Yasmine and Jose sit with Maria at the table and roll balls of play-dough. Maria looks over and says, "Gabriella, want to play with us?" Gabriella continues to track Maria's movements with her eyes, but does not smile or talk. Maria moves across the yard to check on Hector, who has fallen off his bike. Gabriella follows behind her with a serious look on her face. She stands and watches Maria cuddle Hector, looking sad herself. Maria says, "Hey, Gabriella, Hector fell off his trike. His knee hurts. He is crying." Gabriella continues to stand beside Maria as Hector gives Maria a hug and runs over to play on the slide. Maria stands up, holds out her hand to Gabriella, and says, "Want to go inside with me to get a snack?" Gabriella nods yes and tentatively puts her hand in Maria's. They go inside the center.

By tracking Maria, keeping her eye on her and following her, Gabriella demonstrates attachment behaviors. Her behaviors function to keep her physically close to Maria. She is cautious and a bit timid, but able to positively respond to Maria's overtures. Maria also is tracking Gabriella, keeping an eye on her as she negotiates her first day in the center. She gives Gabriella real choices: "Want to play with us?" "Want to go inside?" and follows Gabriella's lead in initiating touch. Maria is able to observe Gabriella and begins to plan how she will work to construct a positive relationship with her.

Our second study was designed to examine relationship formation in the therapeutic preschool (Howes & Ritchie, 1998). Most of the children who are served in this program have been asked to leave one or more child-care settings. Previous teachers and administrators had found the children's aggression, depression, inability to use adults for solace or guidance, poor peer interactions, and frequent flights into disorganized behavior disturbing and disruptive. Furthermore, many children who enter the therapeutic preschool are struggling with difficult life circumstances outside school. They have experienced poverty; disorganized, violent, or chaotic households; and multiple home placements. Many of the children are diagnosed with attachment disorders, oppositional defiant disorders, or posttraumatic stress disorder. About half of the children were prenatally exposed to drugs. As a result of their experiences in and out of school, the children entered the therapeutic preschool with little or no expectation that teachers could be trusted to help them organize their behavior or be emotional resources.

On this day, both Sarah and Henry are new to the therapeutic preschool. Last week they visited the school with their foster mothers. Today, the mothers are watching through the one-way window. Diane, the head teacher, and Marsha, her assistant, have six "old" children plus the two new ones.

Henry begins the morning clinging to Diane. Diane moves around the room chatting with children who are working at the two activity tables. Henry dogs her footsteps, almost attached to her leg. At each table Diane tells Henry who the children are and what they are doing.

Marsha says, "Five minutes to rug time." With help from Diane and Marsha, the "old" children begin to clean up. Sarah has spent the entire morning crouched behind the rocking chair. Whenever a teacher or another child came near her, she averted her face. Marsha goes over to Sarah and says, "It is time for rug time, come with me. I will help you come to rug time." Sarah resists at first softly and then with more volume.

Marsha gently touches her shoulder and says, "Come with me, we are going to be with the class, we are going to rug time." Slowly, Marsha guides Sarah over to the rug and sits close to her. Meanwhile, Diane is playing the autoharp and singing. Henry rests his body against hers. Lilly, an "old" child, sits close on the other side of Diane and sings with her.

Helping Henry and Sarah and the other therapeutic-preschool children to construct positive secure child-teacher attachments is a challenge. The intervention program offered the children a low child-teacher ratio, careful attention to organization and consistency, and an emphasis on building positive and supportive relationships between children and their teachers. The classroom philosophy is based on the idea that the classroom is a community in itself. Each member is valued individually, but also is considered an integral member of the group. Within the program it is important that each child has a voice in the group, learns to listen to others, and takes turns contributing with respect to the others' ideas and feelings.

In our studies of children at the therapeutic preschool, we examined the formation of child-teacher attachment relationships in 31 children. As is true in most early intervention, only one third of the children were girls. We assessed child-teacher relationships using the AQS every 6 months while the children were enrolled. The children in this study remained at the school from 7 to 29 months. Children who remained for two school terms or longer were likely to construct secure child-teacher attachment relationships. Children who were initially diagnosed with an oppositional defiant disorder and remained in school for a shorter period of time were likely to maintain a resistant child-teacher attachment organization. Over time, children moved toward more secure child-teacher relationships and were unlikely to maintain disorganized, near secure, or avoidant attachment organizations. This is a very encouraging study because it suggests that with enough time spent with dedicated reflective teachers, the quality of child-teacher relationships can improve even for children who are extremely troubled and troubling.

Teacher as Organizer and Then Partner

In asserting that school can be different from home, we are saying that children can have an insecure home attachment organization and a secure school attachment organization. To understand how teachers can help children begin to trust when those children enter their classrooms mistrusting them, we need to return to attachment theory and discuss how children use adults to construct attachment relationships (Bowlby, 1982). As infants and toddlers, children use their attachment figures to physically organize their worlds. Normally developing, securely attached toddlers will alternate between moving out into the world to explore new things and people and returning to their adult attachment figure to check in. In this way their attachment figure helps them to explore an exciting and, at times, scary world. Through these experiences toddlers make sense of their world and are able to learn from it. Older children are able to move beyond this organizing stage to what Bowlby (1982) called a goal-directed partnership. Within this partnership children can move to solve life and learning problems without immediate physical help from the adult. When the children are in a partner stage, they can symbolically use their attachment figure. We believe that children who enter classrooms with insecure attachment organizations at home will be helped to move toward secure attachment organizations if the teacher first acts as an organizer rather than as a partner. For teachers of older children this may involve thinking about, and treating, the child as younger than her or his chronological age.

For very young children, using the adult as organizer usually involves keeping the adult in physical proximity. Young children want to know that when they look up from play and exploration, their teacher will be nearby. In older, school-age children, the adult can organize the child in a symbolic, less proximal fashion. Children want to know that the teacher will acknowledge their work, will answer their questions, and will help solve problems. For children who have not been able to consistently predict or count on responses from the adults in their lives, a positive and consistent teacher, functioning as an organizer, can guide them toward self-regulation. In the following narratives, the teacher, functioning as an organizer, assured the children that she could be trusted to notice and respond positively and then helped the children to rejoin the classroom activities.

Jayne's first-grade teacher notices that during a group project on "drawing our neighborhood," Jayne has stopped working within her group and is crying. Without halting the ongoing activity, the teacher stops by Jayne's desk, touches her shoulder, and says, "I can see that you are crying. I'll wait in the classroom so we can talk at recess. Right now you need to be helping with the project." Jayne remains quiet, but manages to control her tears and to attend to the other children's suggestions about the project.

As the group project continues, Max begins talking loudly and shoves his seatmate. The teacher catches his eye, moves so that she is beside him, and says in a strong, but quiet, voice, "Max, I'm going to sit beside you and help you because the group can't do its work if you shout and shove." With the teacher sitting beside him, Max is able to control his voice and body. He suggests that the children draw a market on one of the streets because his grandma lets him walk to the market to get milk.

Notice that the teacher needed to use different behaviors to function as an organizer for these two, very different children. Jayne tends to be "too quiet." She withdraws from the teacher and the other children, acting anxiously vigilant (Cassidy & Berlin, 1994). It was important for the teacher to communicate with Jayne about her emotions. These types of interactions can move Jayne toward a more secure child-teacher attachment relationship. At the same time, the teacher needed to not let Jayne's distress interfere with the learning of the entire group. Jayne cries frequently, and the teacher has found that it works better to speak with her later then to respond to each incident as it occurs. Max fits the description of an exuberant child (Gunnar et al., 1997). It would be easy for Max and his teacher to develop a hostile, conflictual relationship. As a result of the teacher's gently but firmly intervening and then remaining as a physically proximal organizer of Max's behavior, Max does not interfere with his or other children's learning.

When children have moved into the partnership stage of attachment relationships, the teacher no longer must provide all of the classroom structure, but can engage with the children in negotiating classroom rules and routines. When the children's child-teacher relationships are in the partnership stage, there can be more joint construction of learning experiences between the teacher and the children.

The following two narratives illustrate movement from teacher as organizer to goal-directed partnership in Ms. Accardian's kindergarten classroom. The first narrative, with teacher as organizer, occurred during the fall; the second, with teacher as partner, occurred in the spring.

The children are engaged at activity tables. Justin and Jeron are working at an art table. Justin and Jeron are fighting over a pair of scissors. Justin shouts, "That's my scissors. I took it first." Jeron responds, "No, its mine." Ms. Accardian rushes over to the two children and says calmly, "Give me the scissors. We only have one scissors and two people. How do we solve that?" Both children let go of the scissors and hand them to Ms. Accardian. Ms. Accardian gives the scissors to Jeron. Jeron brandishes the scissors in the air, narrowly missing Justin. Ms. Accardian takes the scissors from Jeron, then gives them back, and says, "Now, I want you to go there (pointing across the room) and bring me the scissors back in a safe way." Jeron takes the scissors, holds them safely, walks to the area indicated by Ms. Accardian, and walks back holding the scissors safely.

This is the beginning of the year in a classroom where the learning environment requires that 30 children work independently at learning centers. Ms. Accardian's first priority is making sure that no one gets hurt. She moves quickly to organize children's behavior around safety.

Four months later in the school year, we recorded the following narrative in Ms. Accardian's classroom. Her attachment relationships with the children had developed toward secure, goal-directed partnerships. At this point in the school year she seldom plays a directive organizing role, but continues, as in this narrative, to monitor the children.

Ms. Accardian has set up an activity table called the "Compassion Book" table. The table has paper and pencils on it, and children have been told how to make their books. Four children are busy drawing. Ms. Accardian is close by, observing the activity, but does not engage with the children until the very end. The narrative begins as Justin, sounding as though he is going to cry, says, "You hurt my feelings." Susan asks, "What happened?" Justin says, "She hurt my feelings," and points at Amy. Amy makes noises: "Bah, bah, bahhh." Susan asks in a soft voice, "She did?" Dan asks Justin, "What happened?" Justin says, "She hurt my feelings on purpose." Amy shakes her head no, and says, "As–aa." Justin says, "She hurt my feelings. She said I was scrawling and scribbling." Dan says, "Everyone's drawing is different, just like I draw different than her (pointing at Susan), and she draws different than anybody else. So do you, so do I, and so does anybody else." Ms. Accardian says, "I see how you guys are solving the problem; thank you."

Other narratives and our AQS observations from Ms. Accardian's classrooms suggest that the majority of the children in her classroom constructed secure relationships with her. At this point in the year she can observe and monitor without preventative intrusion into the children's conflict resolution. The Compassion Book activity is part of her ongoing practices to recognize feelings. She has worked as a coach to help children talk about feelings. The "rewards" of this work come in hearing statement's like Dan's "Everyone's drawing is different, just like I draw different than her . . . , and she draws different than anybody else. So do you, so do I, and so does anybody else."

This analysis suggests that especially for children who have difficult prior relationship histories, teachers need to be proactive in organizing children's behaviors in the classroom. This may mean changing the interactive style that early childhood teachers may have become comfortable with. For example, we suspect that if Ms. Accardian had been less directive in the fall, for example, explaining rules of sharing and equity, rather than didactically teaching safe handling of sharp objects, she would not have been as successful in the long run. Assuming that all preschool children are ready to be partners in a relationship negates many children's previous experiences within distrusting relationships.

HOW CAN TEACHERS BE SUPPORTED AND HELPED TO CONSTRUCT SECURE CHILD-TEACHER RELATIONSHIPS?

In the remaining chapters of this book we will continue to describe and analyze our observations of teachers who are struggling with the task of constructing positive relationships with children in their classes. In this section we want to raise several notes of caution. The task of disconfirming children's previous insecure attachment organizations is challenging. It requires from the teacher hard work over long periods of time. Moreover, there are no "quick fixes" and magic solutions to this work. Unlike some other researchers who present frameworks for classroom management (e.g., Bergin & Bergin, 1999; Canter, 1988; Gartell, 1997), we cannot offer a set of exercises or predetermined solutions. The process of disconfirming old relationship patterns and constructing new relationships depends on careful observation and listening to children and on a teacher's reflecting on her or his own practice, examining missteps, and trying again.

We wrote this book to help teachers understand and apply attachment theory. However, an understanding of theory does not necessarily easily lead to an application to practice, nor can practice be successfully implemented without an understanding of theory. Implementing the practices described here requires careful thought and a dedication to a process that is slow and demands consistency over time. Although not produced by a quick fix, the results can be deeply rooted and are worth the effort that is required. Both children and teachers can learn new ways of interacting that can positively serve them in the future.

Research on relationship-based intervention designed to improve child-adult relationships by applying the principles of attachment theory (Erickson & Kurz-Riemer, 1999; Lieberman, Weston, & Pawl, 1991; van IJzendoorn, Juffer, & Duyvesteyn, 1995) suggests that adults can be helped to become more sensitive and responsive and as a result the relationships that they construct with children are more secure. These interventions are most successful when the agents of intervention—in the case of teachers, their mentors and supervisors—build positive relationships with the adults who care for children. As these caregiving adults experience, in some cases for the first time, a positive relationship, they change their own relationship attitudes and behaviors. When the adults reflect on these changes, they can move to understand and enact different practices with children.

Mentoring and reflective supervision may be especially important in relationship-based intervention with teachers because a central component of attachment theory is the concept that all of us, adults as well as children, develop new relationships and are able to learn from others based on our internal working model of relationships (Berlin & Cassidy, 1999). There is ample evidence to suggest that the quality of caregivers' own internalized models of relationships are influential in shaping their relationships with children (Berlin & Cassidy, 1999). Thus teachers who themselves have internalized models of insecure attachment relationships may have difficulty applying attachment theory to practice.

To be effective, relationship-based interventions require that adults rework their strategies of relating to others. Attachment theory holds that internal working models established early in life are difficult, but not impossible, to change. Research on relationship-based intervention suggests that, as noted earlier, intervention was most effective when the caregiving adults had strong, positive relationships with the agents of intervention (Erickson & Kurz-Riemer, 1999; Lieberman et al., 1991). A positive intervener-teacher relationships has these components:

- Ensuring continuity of intervener
- Being consistent and persistent in following through
- Recognizing the teachers' observations and insights as valuable
- Supporting the teacher in finding solutions rather than offering instructions
- Providing emotional and social support for changing behavior

SUMMARY

There is ample evidence that teachers can construct new child-teacher attachment relationships that are different from children's prior relationships. However, this may not be easy for teachers to accomplish without mentoring and reflective supervision. Our observations supported by attachment theory suggest that teachers (as well as other caregiving adults) tend to be reactive. That is, they easily fall into maladaptive patterns of interacting with difficult children. In order to disconfirm maladaptive interactions, teachers must be able to think about why the patterns of behavior are occurring and consciously work to change them. Mentor and reflective supervision appear to help teachers become aware of the processes of interaction and to develop different and proactive strategies.

It appears that when many children meet new teachers, they expect that this new teacher will take care of them. We observed that teachers might need to first organize the children's experiences of relationship building and then engage in a partnership with the children. We observed that among the effective strategies used by teachers of children who have had difficult prior relationships was that of treating them as if they were developmentally younger than their chronological age. That is, in order to disconfirm prior problematic relationship history, teachers constructed new and more positive child-teacher relationships by acting as organizers. As the relationship quality improved, teachers moved to acting as mutually reciprocal partners.

5

Teacher Behaviors that Foster Positive Child–Teacher Relationships

In attempting to understand how teachers can construct positive and secure relationships with the children in their classrooms, we again rely on evidence from research and from analysis of our narrative studies. Using this evidence we have identified categories of teacher behaviors that are associated with constructing both positive and secure child-teacher relationships and classrooms in which all children can learn.

We need to repeat our caution of the previous chapter. While we have identified teacher behaviors that were associated with positive child-teacher relationships, we are not suggesting that these same behaviors would produce a positive relationship between all teachers and all children in all contexts. There are many particular behaviors that can constitute positive, sensitive, responsive behavior to particular children at particular times in the development of the relationship. It is also important to note that the children and teachers in these narratives are primarily people of color and the children often have a home language that is not the language of the school. We have translated all the narratives into English—in doing so we may have missed some nuances.

POSITIVE, SENSITIVE, RESPONSIVE, AND INDIVIDUALIZED ATTENTION

Researchers who study children and their teachers in community-based child-care settings find that teachers who are rated as sensitive and positively involved with the children construct secure child-teacher attachment (Howes & Hamilton, 1992; Kontos, Howes, Galinsky, & Shin, 1994). These findings are consistent with a large and well-established body of research on mother-child attachment relationships that finds that warm, responsive, and sensitive mothers construct secure mother-child attachments with their children (Bretherton, 1985).

Teachers who are warm, sensitive, and responsive not only show warmth and sensitivity in their interactions with the children, but also individualize their responses. Individualized responsiveness to children requires that the teacher observe and reflect on her interactions with each child in the classroom. Novice teachers may believe that being the same way with each child in order to avoid favoritism is important. We suggest that, in contrast, we suggest that expert teachers are sufficiently flexible to individualize their interactions.

Individualized warm, sensitive, and responsive interactions with children tend to do two things. First, such interaction disconfirms the difficult child's working model of child-adult relationships. If the teacher does not reject a child, or behave in an inconsistent manner, but instead acts as if the child is part of the group of children who will form a respectful community, the child's working model of relationships simply does not work. The teacher is not playing her or his part in the exchange. Second, when the teacher is consistent and positive, the child begins to trust that she or he will continue to be so. With this trust and with the disconfirming of established patterns of interaction, the child and teacher are able to construct a new and different relationship. Once this is established, there may be modification of the child's working model of relationships.

Variations in Warm and Individualized Responses

The following narratives illustrate that warm and individualized responsiveness on the part of the teacher can take many different forms.

> Ms. Pattier, a second-grade teacher, is going around checking homework and making notes on her clipboard. When she gets to Evelyn, Evelyn says that she can't find her homework. In a warm but firm tone, Ms. Pattier invokes a class rule and says, "I'll be seeing you at recess." ·
>
> Ms. Pattier moves throughout the classroom and comes upon Juan, who has not completed the homework. She says, "I know you'll bring it tomorrow; let's not have this problem again."
>
> Evelyn protests, "Well why do I have to stay in when he doesn't?"
> Ms. Pattier replies, "Evelyn, I can't give you a break today because you missed your homework for three days in a row."

In this narrative, although Ms. Pattier is not pleased with Evelyn missing homework she is warm, not punitive or harsh, and she explains why Evelyn has to stay in during recess. "Evelyn, I can't give you a break today because you missed your homework for three days in a row." When children cannot stay after school because of busing and parents' nontraditional work schedules, and when a teacher has 30 children of whom many do not have parents home at homework time, recess becomes a time for getting to know a child in a one-to-one setting, finding out what is going on at home, and giving some individualized attention.

In a kindergarten classroom, the children are busy making bear masks for a parade. Ana has stopped her work. Ms. Banks intervenes by asking questions. She is thus able to understand why Ana is off-task and help her move back into a learning context.

> Ana is sitting at a table looking at her mask dejectedly. Ms. Banks kneels next to her and says, "What's the matter, Ana? Are you having trouble?" Ana looks at her sadly with tears in her eyes and says something softly. Ms. Banks looks at her tenderly and says, "We will have many bears in the parade, Ana, but you will be unique because you will be our leopard. Can I help you cut out some spots to put on your mask?" Ana looks up at her and slightly smiles, picking up some black paper to use for spots.

In these narratives both teachers are observant. Ms. Pattier notices that Evelyn has not brought homework for several days and presumably uses this as a cue of a potential problem—in comprehension or at home. We can only speculate what happens at recess time with Ms. Pattier and Evelyn. Ms. Banks notices when Ana's sadness overwhelms her learning activity. Instead of rushing to reprimand, she further investigates. We cannot hear what Ana said or know why a leopard is more satisfying than a bear, but Ana, with the support from Ms. Banks, returns to the activity. In this case learning is extended as a result of the teacher intervention, and the child expresses warmth toward the teacher. Imagine a very different scenario if Ms. Banks had singled out Ana by writing her name on the board or taken time from her recess.

Circle Time as a Routine Context

The setting for the following several narratives is circle time. Circle time helps children feel part of a group, can be a valuable time for building community, and teaches children about listening. But circle time in preschool and kindergarten is also often hard for children. They are asked to sit in one place, share the teacher's attention, and listen to others. Children who have problems with regulation and control and who are preoccupied with their relationship with the teacher have trouble following these routines. In all of the following narratives the teacher's tone is warm, friendly, and firm. She never sounds angry and her tone and words do not reject the children, even as she is working to change their behavior.

In the first two narratives, the teacher, Ms. Rosen, moves fairly quickly to physically assist the child. In each case the child is held on the teacher's lap, but the meaning of the lap sitting is different for each child-teacher dyad. In the first narrative Ms. Rosen uses her body contact to reassure the child of her warm feelings for him even as he moves away. In the second narrative her lap is used as a way to help a child attend to the circle activities when the child cannot regulate her own behavior in order to so.

Tim, a child classified as having an avoidant attachment relationship with Ms. Rosen, is sitting on her lap. He struggles to move away. Ms. Rosen gently pulls him closer. He continues to squirm. Ms. Rosen says to him, "Tim, I want you to be right by me here so you can be part of the group." Tim stops struggling and begins to participate in the group.

Elissa, a child classified as having an ambivalent/resistant attachment relationship with Ms. Rosen, has her body turned around so that she is facing out rather than into the circle. Ms. Rosen says, "Elissa, turn around." Elissa ignores Ms. Rosen. Ms. Rosen says, "Do you need help?" Elissa shakes her head, and continues to face the wrong way. Ms. Jones, the assistant teacher, says, "I'm going to help you. I'm going to have to give Elissa a lap." Elissa says, "No," turns around for about 30 seconds, and then faces the wrong way once more. Ms. Rosen says, "I'm not giving any more chances." She pulls Elissa on to her lap. Elissa sits quietly on Ms. Rosen's lap and holds her hand.

In the next narrative a child who is not attending to circle is worked with over a distance, rather than the teacher removing or containing him. Max is given a choice about staying in or leaving the circle. He stays. Once he has decided to stay, the teacher, Ms. Hardy, keeps in contact with him to help him through the structure of circle time. She works to keep him focused on the content of circle, rather than be drawn into a personal interaction with him.

Max, a child classified as having an ambivalent/resistant attachment relationships with his teacher, Ms. Hardy, is trying to squeeze into a spot in the circle where there is no room. Ms. Hardy says, "Max, move over. There is no space." Max says, "But I don't want to be . . . " Ms. Hardy responds, "Well then leave the rug." Max moves over. Ms. Hardy says, "Good, I'm glad you could find a spot." There is a lot of general noise as children settle into the circle. Max yells, "Let me talk!" Ms. Hardy says, "Stop, no talking, everyone needs to stop. We're going to start our guessing bag. Max, are you ready? I want you to turn your body around so that you'll know when it is your turn."

> Several children take their turn with the guessing bag, and then Ms. Hardy begins to explain the next activity of the day. Max begins talking about toys, which is clearly off the topic. Ms. Hardy says, "Listen, Max, so you will know what the plan is." Max continues to chatter about toys. Ms. Hardy repeats, "Listen, Max, so you will know what the plan is." Max continues to talk about toys. Ms. Hardy says, "No, Max, we are not talking about toys." Circle time ends by a child leader pointing to children who are ready and then dismissing them. By this time Max has wandered away from the circle. He returns, sits down, and says, "Ms. Hardy, I'm ready." Ms. Hardy says, "I'm glad you could do that, Max."

In the next narrative, Ms. Accardian almost ignores a child, Justin, who is disruptive in circle time, as she continues instead with the learning content of the circle. Justin was classified as having an avoidant attachment with her.

> Justin spends the majority of circle time nudging and pushing the child beside him. This child does not say anything to Justin or to Ms. Accardian. After circle time Ms. Accardian puts her arm around Justin and pulls him into what appears to be a quiet but intense conversation.

Instead of carrying on a prolonged engagement with Justin during circle time, Ms. Accardian chooses to work with him individually when the other children do not compose an audience. What occurs in this narrative is quite unlike Ms. Accardian's usual pattern, which is to bring children's peer conflicts immediately into the discussion of the circle; thus is illustrative of individualized responsiveness. We speculate that Ms. Accardian may have taken this opportunity to have a one-on-one interaction with a child who is likely to avoid contact.

TEACHER BEHAVIORS

From our classroom narratives, we identified teacher behaviors that function to provide children with positive, sensitive, responsive, and individualized attention. These behaviors include

- Teacher talk
- Giving warnings before transitions and new experiences
- Validating children's experiences and feelings
- Being involved in learning with children
- Being consistent and firm
- Making a plan

- Avoiding power struggles
- Supporting children's positive behaviors and learning
- Maintaining high expectations
- Providing positive attention

In the following sections we elaborate and give examples of each of these behaviors.

TEACHER TALK

Teachers demonstrate to children that they can be predictably trusted through their use of language. The teachers in our observations used the same phrases over and over again. The content of phrases, as well as the repetition, appeared to help the children trust the teachers. With their words, the teachers conveyed to the children that they were worthy of affection, and that the teachers were available to help the children.

Teachers in our observations told children that they were available to help when a child was having a difficult time. The words "I'm going to help you" indicated to the children that the teacher could be trusted to keep them safe.

During a cleanup routine in the therapeutic preschool, Tim runs across the room away from the tables of toys to be cleaned up. Ms. Rosen picks Tim up. He struggles against her. Ms. Rosen says, "I'm going to help you. You can play with the train later. It is time to put the toys away." Tim moves close to another child, intruding on her space. Ms. Rosen continues, "I'm going to help you. I'm going to stop you. You may not hit Carolyn. Put the toys away and help clean up the tables." Ms. Rosen steps between the two children and helps them to put away the toys.

During circle time Ben wiggles and squirms. Ms. Jones says, "I'm going to help you. I'm going to give you a lap."

Diego climbs up to a table during activity time. Ms. Garcia says, "Diego, get down from that table. Do you need me to help you get down?"

When children hear the same phrase repeated, and when the teacher has been successful in using the phrase in contexts that help children to trust her, she can then use it to reassure children. The following narrative illustrates the use of "I'm going to help you" both to guide Carolyn's behavior and to reassure Chrissie that the teachers could be trusted to keep everyone safe in school.

During free play, Chrissie and Ms. Rosen have been playing with the babies. Carolyn dumps the doll clothes on the rug. Chrissie goes to get the doll clothes. Carolyn screams, "NO, NO, NO, NO!" Ms. Rosen says, "Wait a minute, Carolyn and Chrissie. It is to share. Work it out. Carolyn, pass it to Chrissie." Carolyn goes to push Chrissie. Ms. Rosen says, "There is no pushing. You know that, Carolyn. It is to share." Carolyn looks angry and throws the doll clothes. Ms. Rosen says, "I'm going to help you pick up the ones you threw." Carolyn picks up the doll clothes without help, but still refuses to let Chrissie have any. Ms. Rosen says, "So hand it to her, or I'll help you." Carolyn dumps out all the rest of the doll clothes, screams, and hits Chrissie. Ms. Rosen says, "You're done in this area, hitting is not OK," and asks the assistant teacher to take Carolyn to another part of the room. Ms. Rosen holds Chrissie and says, "I know that hurts. Ms. Jones is going to help Carolyn. She'll be OK. Are we going to feed the babies?"

Other phrases that the teachers we observed used repeatedly were "I'm going to say no because . . ." and "I'm going to stop you because . . ." Such phrases served to alert children that the teacher was going to intervene in their behavior to help them stop themselves. It also provided a reason for the teacher's intervention. The use of the phrase "I'm going to" serves to give the children a warning and the choice to stop themselves before the teacher intervenes. The following narratives illustrate the use of this phrase.

It is morning activity time. Henry grabs a playdough toy away from Carolyn. Carolyn protests loudly, "No!" Ms. Jones says, "You know, Henry, Carolyn doesn't want you to take her things." Henry grabs another toy. Carolyn shouts, "No!" and grabs the toy back. Ms. Jones responds to Henry, "You know, I'm going to stop you. I'm going to say no. We have only one of those." Henry cries, "I want what Carolyn has. I want what Carolyn has." He touches Carolyn's toy again. Ms. Jones says, "I'm going to say no; that is not OK to take her toys." She continues, "Are you worried that you are not going to get toys to play with? There are lots of toys and all the children are sharing."

During cleanup, Max is crashing into Maria. Neither child is helping with cleanup. Ms. Hardy says, "Maria and Max, crashing your bodies isn't going to work. I'm going to stop you, Max, until you can stop your body." Ms. Hardy guides Max to a chair and has him sit down.

During snack, Randy is singing Halloween songs. Ms. Ryan says, "I'm going to say the singing should stop so that we can finish snack."

Both the phrase "I'm going to help you" and the phrases "I'm going to say no/I'm going to stop you" also are illustrations of the teacher as organizer in the development of an attachment relationship. As the child-teacher relationships of the children in our observed classrooms moved toward the goal-directed partnership stage of attachment-relationship formation, teacher talk changed. Teachers *asked* the children instead of telling them. The following narratives illustrate teacher talk when the children are asked rather than told.

> During cleanup time Henry leaves the Legos and wanders away. Ms. Rosen calls to him, "Henry, we've got to put those away first." Henry first ignores Ms. Rosen. Then he returns and works with Ms. Rosen to put the Legos in the bin. Before the job is finished, Henry takes off across the room, leaving the cleanup task unfinished. Ms. Rosen says to him, "We've got to finish. Come back. We're not done. Either come back, or I'm going to stop you." In response, Henry dumps out the entire bin of Legos. Ms. Rosen says, "Now you really have a big job. Now you have more to do. Do you want me to help or do you want to do it yourself?" Henry responds, "I don't want help." He finishes cleaning up on his own.

> Several of the children are playing in a small outdoor playground. One of the walls of the playground is made up of the windows to an activity room. The children are very interested in climbing up on some steps and watching other children working with a teacher in the room. Ms. Braun walks over to them and asks, "What is happening here?" Sean responds, "I'm watching the children." Ms. Braun says, "Yes, it is very interesting, but it bothers them while they work. Come on down." Sean continues to watch. Ms. Braun repeats, "Come on down now, make a different choice." Sean comes down and wanders over to push a large ball. In a few moments he returns and climbs up the steps to watch once again. Ms. Ryan, another teacher on the yard, walks over to him and says, "What did Ms. Braun say?" Sean responds, "No." He comes down off the steps and begins to play elsewhere. He does not return to the windows.

A second developmental change in teacher talk involved teachers modeling information gathering and then having children come up with problem-solving solutions on their own. In the following narrative, children in Ms. Accardian's classroom had been playing together with a toy shark. The play starts out being cooperative, but after a few minutes, there is a disagreement over the ownership of the shark. The children each try to take the shark from the other.

Bob says, "I'm telling," and gets up and starts running across the room toward Ms. Accardian. Juan runs after Bob, grabbing at his arm, trying to stop him. Ms. Accardian has been supervising another activity. She stops immediately and says to Bob and Juan, "Wait, stop, stop. First of all, do you know what I saw? Two people not being safe with each other. That's the first thing I saw. Could you tell me what happened?" The children both talk at the same time, and no one can hear what the other is saying. Ms. Accardian bends down and places a hand on each child's shoulder. She says, "You know what, let's go solve this problem. What's the problem?" Bob looks at Ms. Accardian and says, "Well, well, see he wouldn't let me play with his animal, but I—" Juan interrupts. "He took the shark over here and he was playing with them all the time and uh. . . ." Ms. Accardian continues, "And then you wanted to play with it, right?" Juan says, "Yeah, I did." Ms. Accardian continues, "Did you ask him in a nice voice, 'Can I play with it, Bob?' And what did Bob say?" Bob answers, "Um, well, I said I wanted to play for a little while." Ms. Accardian says, "OK, and then did you play with it for a little while?" Bob says, "Well, well, I was playing with it and he said no. . . ." Ms. Accardian says, "Oh, Juan said no afterwards. OK, you know what, let's figure out how to fix that."

Bob turns and walks away. Ms. Accardian says in a very firm voice "Bob, Bob, we are not finished. Do not move from here until I say so, OK?" Bob returns. Ms. Accardian turns Bob gently so that he is fully facing her. "So what do we do about this? What would you like Bob to know for next time?" Juan responds, "Don't scratch me." Bob defends, "I didn't." Juan starts to cry, "Yes, you did." Bob protests, "No, no, you scratched me." Ms. Accardian interrupts. "Bob, you know what, Bob? He is giving you information you need to keep in mind. He says don't scratch next time. And if you want him to know the same thing, tell him."

Several months later, again in Ms. Accardian's classroom, we observed the children gathering information and attempting to problem solve without the immediate guidance of Ms. Accardian. Juan and Ted are in the midst of painting and they run into each other. Juan does not seem to be aware that he has pushed Ted, and Ted does not seem to be bothered by the contact. However, Mario, who has observed the incident, accuses Juan of pushing Ted. Juan denies the pushing, but Mario persists and sends Ted off to tell Ms. Accardian. The following narrative illustrates the bystanders Mario, Jill, and Mike gathering information and attempting to solve the problem.

Mike leans toward Juan and Mario and says, "What did Juan say happened?" Juan responds, "I didn't push him." Mike says, "Without saying excuse me?" Mario nods vigorously. "Yeah, without saying excuse me." Sounding angry,

Juan says, "I didn't do it. What do you mean, guys?" Mike says, "Look, Ted's gone. You can't even see him. He's not gonna be your friend." Jill joins in. "He didn't say that, remember." Mario says, "But I told Ted to tell on you because you tell on people."

Ted returns with Ms. Accardian, who says, "You know what, we don't tell on people. You know that, right? We solve our problems. We look at each other and talk about it. OK, Mario, what was the problem you had? And Juan, what would you like Mario to know for next time?"

Over time, teacher talk becomes another means by which children learn to expect their teachers to be predictable. For children whose prior experiences with adults have been chaotic and disorganized, such talk serves as an organizer of interaction and, eventually, relationships. For other children, teacher talk becomes a guide for solving conflicts and resolving problems.

Giving Warnings Before Transitions and New Experiences

Warnings before transitions and new experiences give children the opportunity to come to a stopping place in their learning experience and anticipate controlling their behavior. Warnings occur when teachers give clear explanations of upcoming experiences and let children know when something may be different or new. Often the teachers we observed would anticipate possible responses to a new experience and narrate them to the children so the children would have some strategies for managing and controlling their own behavior.

In the following narrative, it is the first week of kindergarten for 5-year-old Andrew. Ms. Bateman provides Andrew with a warning about classroom routines, which helps him participate with the rest of his group.

Andrew is still eating his snack after recess has ended. Ms. Bateman says, "Andrew, are you going to be done soon so you can join us?" Andrew nods vigorously, shoves the rest of his Doritos in his mouth, and sits on the rug.

Ms. Mack's first-grade class has been counting to 56 by fives while jumping on both feet, doing jumping jacks, doing push-ups, and standing in the tree trunk pose. They are quite excited that they have accomplished this task and are all out of their seats. Ms. Mack provides a warning before the class transitions to a less vigorous activity.

Ms. Mack tells the class to get ready for newsletter time and to think of things they want to share. She lets Juliana know that she will be the first to share news. All the children settle into their seats while Ms. Mack gets out the paper and clips it to the board. She then turns to Juliana, who offers her news.

At the end of recess Ms. Mack welcomes the children back into the classroom. The children enter the room and sit in their rug spots. Ms. Mack tells them to sit in their seats because it is phonics time. Most of the children head for their seats. Two children get the phonics notebooks out of storage.

Giving warnings is another way that teachers became trustworthy and predictable. Warnings are especially supportive when they serve to proactively help children manage and control their own behavior.

Validating Children's Experiences and Feelings

In preceding chapters we have discussed the value of validating children's emotions in children's development of regulation and control. The teachers we watched validated children's experiences as well as their emotions. Validating children's experiences may be particularly important for children who have come from difficult life circumstances because they may have learned to keep silent about an experience such as homelessness or domestic violence in order to ward off shame or distress.

The teachers we observed acted as if children who are expressing anxiety, sadness, anger, or pain needed to be heard. They are not told, "Don't worry about it," or "It will be OK," or "That's just a little scratch; it doesn't hurt," but rather "That must be scary," "I know that makes you mad," or "I bet that does hurt; let's get a cold cloth."

In the following narrative, Ms. Garcia's kindergarten class is sitting on the carpet for science. Allyson is sitting in the back, cross-legged, and looking relaxed and engaged. Ms. Garcia is reading to the children.

> Ms. Garcia holds up book and asks, "What do you think is going to happen?" Allyson and several other children eagerly chant, "It's gonna grow."
> Ms. Garcia asks, "What does a plant need to grow?" The children respond, "Water." Ms. Garcia puts the book down and asks the class, "What are we going to grow?" Several children respond, "Pumpkins." Allyson has become quiet and subdued. She does not respond to the next four questions about growing pumpkins. Ms. Garcia asks quietly, "Allyson are you going to plant a pumpkin with us?" Allyson responds, "My Daddy smashed my pumpkin and hit me." Ms. Garcia says, "That sounds very scary. Is it hard for you to think about pumpkins?" Allyson nods her head yes. Ms. Garcia continues, "Would you like to keep your pumpkin here? I'll keep it safe for you." Allyson says loudly, "Yes." Ms. Garcia asks the class to move to the table outside to plant the pumpkin seeds.

Ms. Garcia noticed that she had lost Allyson from the exciting discussion of planting pumpkins. By validating Allyson's experiences and feelings ("That sounds very scary. Is it hard for you to think about pumpkins?"), she makes the experience a little bit less shameful. She underlines the validity of Allyson's fears by offering to keep her pumpkin safe, and by extension, she provides a safe space for Allyson.

Being Involved in Learning with Children

When teachers actively *join* children in their play and learning, children come to know that their learning behaviors are respected.

> Ms. Fitch is conducting a sensory-motor activity for the 5-year-olds in her class. They are listening to a tape that requires them to attend carefully to instructions that help them learn the meaning of *around, under, in, over,* and *on.* Most of the children in the class are second-language learners. It is Dante's turn and he is supposed to go "around" the circle. Ms. Fitch watches as Dante hesitates, unsure of what to do. She says, "Think about it carefully . . . aaaaaarrrrrrroound"; she circles her head as she repeats the word. Dante picks up the cue and walks around the circle proudly. Ms. Fitch takes his hand and skips gaily around the circle with him, saying, "I really like the way you took my clue and figured it out all by yourself."

In this example we suspect that Ms. Fitch enjoyed her skipping and playing and being like a child. We can think of other examples, particularly problem-solving tasks or artwork, where the teacher might be genuinely learning new material with the children.

Being Consistent and Firm

Teachers who are consistent and firm follow through. Being consistent and firm does not mean being inflexible. Teachers who are firm and consistent maintain limits once they have been set and do not back down.

> The children in Ms. Snyder's first-grade classroom are working individually at their desks. Ms. Snyder is walking around the room helping children who are struggling. Quelani comes across the room to Ms. Snyder's side, paper in hand, brimming over with things to say. "I can't do this one, will you help me, I think it is wrong." Ms. Snyder interrupts the flow and says, "I'll talk with you when you are in your seat with your hand raised." "But I can't do it, I just want to show you, I can't do it." Ms. Snyder repeats her statement and turns back to the child she was helping. Quelani returns to her seat and raises her hand.

By her unwillingness to respond to Quelani's anxiety, Ms. Snyder helps Quelani to regain her self-control and perhaps to develop some self-reliance. Notice that Ms. Snyder does not reprimand Quelani, and in fact reassures her that she will help her.

> The bell rings for recess in Ms. Horner's second–grade class. Most of the children go to the door to line up. Six of the children remain at their desks. They take out various books and papers and begin to work. Their names are on the board for incomplete work and they know they will not go to recess. This plan is in effect every day. The teacher does not even have to talk about it.

While we may or may not agree with Ms. Horner's rule that leaves some children without recess, it is part of the daily routine. The matter-of-fact behavior of the students may indicate that they have accepted the rule as their responsibility as well as the teacher's.

Making a Plan

> The children come back in from lunch. They are chattering eagerly about their upcoming turn in the auditorium. It is their time to use the mats for tumbling, and they have been looking forward to it all week. Mr. Hernandez calms them down and says, "I have some sad news. Our plan to be in the auditorium for the afternoon has fallen through. The principal told me at lunch that he needs the auditorium for a meeting. I was mad at him because I thought he should have told me earlier. I told him that the children in my class were going to be very disappointed. He apologized to us and said he should have told us earlier, but he said we would have to make a new plan. So now we have two things to do. One is to make a new plan for this afternoon, and the second one is to decide when we will use the auditorium again."

This narrative combines being firm and consistent with another kind of teacher talk, making a plan. The teacher is consistent with his students even when another force has intervened. The use of a plan further assures them that he can be trusted.

Avoiding Power Struggles

> The class is working on their math tests. Daniel throws down his pencil and begins to pace the room, saying, "I'm not gonna do it and you can't make me." Ms. Diaz approaches Daniel and quietly asks him what the problem is. He only repeats, "I'm not gonna do it, and you can't make me." Ms. Diaz has run into these ultimatums with Daniel before. She has found that challenging

him only escalates his behavior, and in fact she cannot make him sit down. She simply says to him, "Either work on it now or we can find a time for you to finish it later." She walks away from him. Daniel does not complete the test, but he sits at his desk and doodles and does not disturb the other students.

Ms. Diaz refrains from engaging in a power struggle when Daniel is upset and the interaction would threaten to flare into a conflict. Note that she has observed Daniel's past behavior (and her response), reflected on it, and developed an individualized response to him.

Supporting Children's Positive Behaviors and Learning

When teachers support children's positive behaviors and learning, they interact in a manner that helps children *continue* with their play, learning, or interactions. These teachers provide children with opportunities for expanded play or learning verbally or with materials. Ms. Taki demonstrates supportive behavior in the following narrative from a first-grade class.

The children's assignment had been to make a shadow drawing of an object and then to write clues about the picture. The children were taking turns presenting their drawings and asking the others to guess what they were. It is Jessica's turn.

Jessica walks to the front and sits on the special presenter's chair. She is both very proud of her work and apprehensive about engaging with the class. Jessica turns her paper around and holds it up. Many children raise their hands. Jessica looks at Ms. Taki, who smiles and nods. Jessica says, "Derek." Derek asks, "Is it a tadpole?" Jessica smiles and shakes her head no. Ms. Taki says, "Oh, we forgot; you haven't told them the clues yet." Jessica reads from the paper, "It has eyes and has fur." Many hands go up. Jessica again visually checks in with Ms. Taki, who smiles. Jessica says, "Monica." Monica guesses: "Cat." Jessica has a really big smile and says, "Yes."

Note in the narrative how often Jessica visually checks in with Ms Taki. In turn Ms. Taki gives Jessica plenty of positive responses.

Maintaining High Expectations

Many children with difficult life circumstances and certainly children who have prior insecure relationships with their teachers believe that teachers think that they will not be able to do well academically or to regulate their behaviors. When teachers have high expectations, they act as if children will do their best, will follow classroom rules, and will behave in a respectful manner.

We observed that only when high expectations were combined with kindness and warmth were they an effective teacher strategy for building positive relationships and disconfirming prior problematic relationship history. The tone of comments; their ritual nature, allowing every student a careful explanation about the quality of her or his work; and the generally positive atmosphere of the classroom provided a context in which high expectations contributed to positive relationship formation.

Providing Positive Attention

Teachers are challenged to provide positive attention to children. When there are 20 or more children in the class, the child who is quietly and happily involved in a learning activity typically receives less attention than the one who is having a tantrum. A recent research project is illustrative (Baker, 1999). Baker studied third- to sixth-grade African American students and their teachers. Besides interviewing the children and the teachers about child-teacher relationships, she observed positive teacher behaviors and reprimands. Children who were dissatisfied with their child-teacher relationships had a 5:11 ratio of reprimands to positive comments—for every positive comment there were more than five reprimands. Children who reported that they were happy with their teachers had a 3:1 ratio of reprimands to positive comments. This study not only illustrates the importance of a lower reprimand-to-positive-comment ratio; it demonstrates how forgiving children can be. The satisfied children were still receiving three reprimands for every positive comment.

In the following narrative, Ms. Armfield offers a positive comment when many teachers would have simply reprimanded Ryan and forbidden the activity.

> Team 1 is drawing the poster that will accompany the kindergarten's Thanksgiving poem. Ryan is drawing people being killed with swords. Dylan and Jennifer G. let out exasperated sighs and walk and run over to Ms. Armfield, who is at the computer table. Dylan says, "Ms. Armfield, Ryan is drawing people getting killed with swords and stuff." Dylan and Jennifer walk away, and Ms. Armfield calls out to Ryan: "Ryan. Come over here." Ryan throws down the two pens he is using and walks over to Ms. Armfield. She says to him, "Ryan, they said you were drawing people getting killed by swords. Is that true? Is that what I'll see if I go over there?" Ryan is quiet. Ms. Armfield says, "You're such a good artist Ryan. . . . " Ryan goes back to the group and colors over what he has drawn.

It sometimes takes a creative teacher to find the positive, and in doing so it is easy to sound phony. Here Ms. Armfield uses a combination of avoiding power stuggles and finding the positive. We suspect that she has been working hard in many different ways to construct a positive relationship with Ryan.

SUMMARY

Certainly the notion that teachers are to be positive, sensitive, and warm is not a new one. The popular-press image of a child-care or early elementary education teacher is of a warm, perhaps motherly, person who loves children and wants to be with them.

While the effective teachers whom we observed could be described as warm and sensitive, they also individualized their interactions with children. We believe that because their interactions with children were individualized and responsive, they were able to establish positive trusting child-teacher relationships. Individualized and responsive interaction is no easy task for teachers who are working with groups of 10 to 30 children. Among the other things that teachers must hold in their minds is their working theory of engagement with many different children, for whom a warm response must be individualized. This working model needs to be constantly revised in light of the everyday interactions of teachers with particular children. Perhaps this is why, as we discussed in Chapter 4, teachers can most effectively learn to engage in this way of teaching when they have a mentor or supervisor with whom they can discuss their interactions with children.

Our narratives illustrate that teachers who were effective in constructing positive child-teacher relationships employed a variety of behaviors or strategies with children. Together these individual strategies reflect warmth and engagement with the children's emotions and life experiences, coupled with consistent behavior and a belief in the importance of high expectations and high achievement. It is tempting to take these behaviors out of context or to suggest that perhaps one set of behaviors is more important than another. However, our observations in these classrooms suggest that it is particular behaviors in the context of particular classroom climates that lead to positive relationships. In the following chapters we will extend our vision to these larger contexts.

6

Classroom Organizations that Foster Positive Child–Teacher Relationships

Ms. Redding says, "Go ahead, Ollie, wash your hands. Get ready for lunch." Ollie remains on the rug. He is peaceful and quiet, but simply not moving. Ms. Redding encourages him once again, and then moves to assist the other children as they bring their lunches to the table. Ollie sits on the rug quietly until the precise time that lunch usually occurred. (This child cannot tell time.) He then gets up, gets his lunch, and joins the group.

In this chapter our primary source of evidence comes from observations from the Children With Difficult Life Circumstances Study. We examined our data, including the narrative above, looking for classrooms that were fostering positive children-teacher relationships in settings with high proportions of children with difficult life circumstances. We identified three categories of classroom organization associated with positive child-teacher relationships: clear, consistent, and predictable routines; stability of the group over lengthy time periods; and a focus on cooperative learning and peer tutoring.

CLEAR, CONSISTENT, AND PREDICTABLE CLASSROOM ROUTINES

Children who live in difficult life circumstances often lead chaotic lives. There may be almost daily changes in where and when the child sleeps; where, what, and when the child eats; and who is taking care of the child. The adult caregivers of these children, for many reasons, are unable to be consistent and predictable in their patterns of responding to and interacting with the child. School can play an important role in the lives of these children simply because it is predictably in one place, starts at the same time every day, and has the same person as teacher every day. Beyond the structure provided by the institution of school, teachers can construct classrooms that are predictable. This predictability serves to disconfirm children's expectations that the world and the adults within it are not to be trusted.

Predictable and consistent classroom routines give the teacher a number of advantages. Once the children understand classroom routines, there are fewer issues to be negotiated. For example, if cleanup time predictably follows free-activity time and if everyday cleanup involves all the children, then once the routine is established, the class is ready for the next activity without conflict or chaos. Predictable and consistent classroom routines also leave less time for uncomfortable transitions. If children and the teacher move smoothly between learning activities, the children do not spend much time aimlessly wandering or endlessly waiting.

Children can use the structure of the classroom to organize themselves. Ollie, the 4-year-old who waited on the rug until his internal clock said it was lunchtime, comes from a home with little in the way of predictable routines. At school, life is more predictable. Because children completing free choice had cleaned up very quickly, perhaps because they now understood the routine, the teachers found that they were going to have to move into lunch a bit early. The children were excused from the rug to wash their hands. But Ollie remained on the rug even though he had been excused. Ms. Redding realized that for Ollie, having a predictable routine was more important than having lunch early. Her response to him was individualized and reflects the importance of predictable routines for children from chaotic homes.

For children who have had little experience with adults who are reliably available and predictable, routines in which the teacher is consistently positive provide them with opportunities to understand that the teacher is to be trusted. From these experiences of trusting the teacher, the child and teacher can construct a positive secure attachment relationship. For children whose previous relationship history has been one of disorganization or of ambivalent/resistant organization, the experience of a positive adult who organizes the child's world in a predictable fashion can serve to disconfirm previous experiences and lead to the construction of more positive adult-child attachment organizations. The following narrative illustrates this process.

In Ms. Hardy's classroom the routine for free-choice time involves children coming to a particular place, the rug; choosing an activity from those available; and then taking a card with their name on it to the activity center. When they are finished in an activity center, they are to return to the rug with their card, and make another choice. In the following narrative, Ms. Hardy uses the structure of the routine to help organize Betty and Randy. By focusing on the routine rather than their disruptive behavior, she redirects them toward learning activities.

> Betty and Randy have chosen pretend play. They are, however, roughhous-ing, which breaks the classroom rule. Ms. Hardy is watching the children, but has not, as yet, commented on their rule breaking. Betty looks at Ms. Hardy and says, "What are you doing?" Ms. Hardy responds, "I'm just watching to see what you are doing because pretend is not a wild place." Betty continues to jump on the pillows. Ms. Hardy says, "Betty, pretend is not a place to bounce around." Randy begins bouncing on the pillows. Ms. Hardy says to both children, "So, put your stuff away and be done. Come to the rug and take your card. What do you want to do in the short time you have left?" Randy goes to the rug and chooses the manipulative toys. Betty is still in the pretend area. She leaves and goes to another activity center and gets out a new toy. Ms. Hardy says, "No, you didn't say anything about sit 'n spin. You need to make a choice on the rug." Ms. Hardy takes Betty's arm and guides her to the rug.

Routines can be particularly important for children with disorganized attachment organization. The following narrative demonstrates how being guided through a cleanup routine appears to help a child who has a disorga-nized attachment organization. In Ms. Rosen's classroom, the routine is that all children participate in cleaning up after free play, rather than each child cleaning up what she or he played with. All children must participate, and teachers do not ignore the children who avoid cleanup. The teachers are willing to go through the tantrum and refusal each time if necessary, in order to remain consistent in their expectations of the children.

> Henry is twirling and spinning across the room, not cleaning up. Ms. Rosen takes his hand and guides him back to the tables. "It's time to clean up, Henry." He breaks away and spins across the room once more. Ms. Rosen says, "Henry, you need to clean up." Henry shouts, "No!" and runs across the room. Ms. Rosen says, "Henry, come on over." She picks him up and brings him back to the table. Ms. Rosen says to Henry, "You need to put that hat in the dress-up corner." Henry takes the hat and goes with it to the dress-up corner. As he runs back to the table he calls out jubilantly, "Ms. Rosen, I did it!" Ms. Rosen responds, "OK, sweetie. Take the playdough and put it over there on the shelf."

The next narrative illustrates how routines, which are not usually in-dividualized, can be combined with individualized attention to children. In Ms. Accardian's classroom, circle time is used as a period in which teachers and children plan and discuss learning activities. On the morning of this ob-servation, Ted wanted Ms. Accardian to vary the routine so that he could communicate something very important to the group. Ms. Accardian both stays with the routine, thus not disrupting the predictable routine for the entire group, and manages to convey to Ted that she can be trusted to take his concerns seriously.

> While Ms. Accardian is talking about the day's cooking project, Ted raises his hand for the second time and then talks without being called on, "I want to tell them something." Ms. Accardian cuts Ted off: "I'm talking right now," and continues to explain the cooking project. Ted frowns, but remains quiet and still. Ms. Accardian begins to dismiss the children for outside play. Children leave when she calls the first letter of their names. Ted raises his hand and starts to speak at the same time as Ms. Accardian. "Ms. Accardian, I want to tell everyone something." Ms. Accardian looks directly at Ted and says, "I'm talking right now, Ted. I need you to hold on to your thought. I can see you really have something to say, OK?" Ted puts his hand down and nods his head. He averts his face. Ms. Accardian continues dismissing children by the letters of their names. When the letter *T* is called, Ted ignores it, and stays seated, even when another child urges him to leave because his letter was called.
>
> When all the children have left, Ms. Accardian turns to Ted and says, "Ted, are you ready to come outside and tell me what you have to say?" Ted says, "I wanted to say it to the whole group." Ms. Accardian says, "Well, we can go to the stoop and you can do that." She walks outside with Ted following her. When all the children have moved outside, are sitting on the stoop, and attending to Ms. Accardian, she says, "Before we go out to play, Ted has something to tell us." Ted stands up and says, "Yeah, it is very, very important." Ms. Accardian says, "Ted, what did you need to tell us?" Ted says, "I don't want anyone touching my clays at the clay table, the big lump of it, because that big one is the dessert I made. It has lots of eggs that are vulture eggs. And you know what, if you touch it, it might be broken some-how. And I don't want it to get broken because it took me like—it took me a very long time. Like 30 minutes to do that. Forty hundred minutes." He sits down. Ms. Accardian says, "Thank you. Now you can all go play."

The preceding narrative illustrates how Ted trusted Ms. Accardian to attend to him. The end of the story suggests that Ted's trust was reasonable; Ms. Accardian could be trusted to listen and to help him tell the others. A narrative recorded 6 months earlier, although not within a routine, gives us some insight into how Ted's trust of Ms. Accardian developed. The narrative begins during dismissal from circle time. All the other children have left the circle and are getting their snack. Ted is still sitting at the circle.

> Ms. Accardian says, "Ted, when you are ready, you come and talk to me." She leaves the circle area. Ted doesn't say anything. Ms. Accardian turns off

the light in the room and goes outside to where the other children are having snack. Ted plays with the tape on the carpet for a few minutes. He then gets his snack and joins the others. Ms. Accardian comes to Ted and says, "When you are ready, you can come and tell me why you are upset." Ted remains quiet. Ms. Accardian looks at Ted and says, "Maybe you can talk to me after you finish your snack."

As in the other narrative, Ted does not act as though he is finished with circle time. Like Ollie, he appears to use the predictability and consistency of classroom routines to organize his emotions and behavior. He does not act in a hostile fashion, but something in his demeanor indicates to Ms. Accardian that he is upset. Ms. Accardian lets him know that she can be trusted with his feelings by making sure that he has a chance to talk with her.

STABILITY OF THE TEACHER AND THE GROUP

It is important to remember that each child-teacher attachment relationship is with a particular teacher. We don't have children who are secure or insecure; we have child-teacher relationships that are secure or insecure. This means that teachers are not interchangeable. A child in a child-care classroom may very well have different patterns of relationships with the morning teacher, the afternoon teacher, and the four assistant teachers. A kindergarten child might have a different type of relationship with the classroom teacher, after-school teachers, playgroup aide, and work-study student who always comes on Thursday and Friday afternoons.

Every time the child experiences a new teacher, the child and the teacher must begin and complete the process of constructing a new relationship. Particularly for very young children, the task of constructing new relationships is easier when there is continuity or consistency in their environment. This is important because they are extracting patterns in order to make sense of their worlds. It's easier if there is consistency across all those patterns of being cared for.

Easier, as we have seen, does not mean better or more positive relationships. If the child experiences consistent responsive caregiving at home and in child care, then that child is likely to have multiple secure attachment relationships, and that is an advantage for the development of social competence (Howes, Rodning, Galluzzo, & Meyers, 1988). We hope, however, that if the child receives neglectful or harmful caregiving in one setting and constructs an insecure relationship, this kind of interaction and relationship construction does not happen across settings. Moreover, we hope that this does not happen across time in school. This brings us to the issue of keeping the same teacher with a group of children over time.

Child-care teachers are less likely to remain with a group of children for a school year than are elementary teachers and hardly ever remain for more than one year (Howes & Hamilton, 1993; Whitebook & Bellm, 1999). This is primarily because child-care teachers' compensation levels are so very low that teachers cannot afford to stay if a better economic opportunity appears. In addition, both child care and school tend to be age graded so that children move to a different classroom and a different teacher each year.

Child-care teachers who stay with the same children for an extended period of time tend to engage in more appropriate, attentive, and engaged interactions with these children than do teachers who spend less time with the children (Raikes, 1993; Whitebook, Howes, & Phillips, 1990). Children who do not have stability and consistency in teachers are more aggressive, are less skilled with peers, and have smaller vocabularies than children who have fewer teacher changes (Howes & Hamilton, 1993; Whitebook et al., 1990). Likewise, there is some emerging evidence that elementary children may benefit from "looping"—an arrangement in which students and teachers persist as a group over several academic years (Grant, Johnson, & Richardson, 1996).

One of the participants in the Children with Difficult Life Circumstances Study was a therapeutic half-day preschool program that keeps children and teachers together for 2 years. Each classroom includes children similar in chronological age and time in school and dissimilar in psychiatric diagnosis at time of entry. Our longitudinal data on these children suggest that the longer the children remain in the school, the more likely it is that they will be able to construct a secure child-teacher relationship (Howes & Ritchie, 1998).

Another program, in the Best Practices Study, is supported by state and federal child-care funds to provide full-day child care for low-income children. The program has a very low teacher-turnover rate, so children keep the same primary teacher the entire time they are in the center. Some of the teachers are now caring for the grandchildren of the first children they taught when they began teaching. Children and their siblings are assigned to the same homeroom. Children never change their room assignments, so the timid 2-year-olds of one year become the future 5-year-old organizers of play. Because of this practice, unrelated as well as related children grow up together.

The outside play area at this program is very large. On a typical day, several groupings of children will be involved in different activities. For example, a group may be riding bikes, another doing water painting on the walls, one playing in the sandbox, another over by the jump rope area, a group on the climbing structures, and a group having their faces painted. There are teachers in some areas, and none in others. There are no rules that say that children have to stay in any particular area, and they have the choice of moving throughout the yard. Despite this, most children remain in their classroom groups, near their teachers. There two exceptions—boys who race throughout the yard in their chase games, and groups of children who make active decisions to move together from one area to another. This narrative follows one of the latter groups.

> A group of 4-year-olds are skipping across the playground, headed for the jump rope area under the big tree in the far corner. A much younger girl tags along. One of the older girls, Esmeralda, glances back, slows down, and takes the hand of the younger girl. It is apparent, if one looks closely, that they are sisters. The children proceed to the jump rope area and begin to take turns jumping and turning the rope. The younger child watches, and when it is her sister's turn to jump, she takes her hand, invites her to join her, and tries to teach her how to jump. None of the other girls object; it appears to be a ritual that they are accustomed to.

When we first began our work with this program, we felt overwhelmed. There are three very large classrooms, each with 65 children and eight teachers. We wondered how positive child-teacher relationships could develop in this setting. We now believe that family groupings with teachers rooted in the school are the key to the many positive child-teacher relationships we observed.

There can be a downside, of course, to spending multiple years with the same teacher—when there is a poor relationship between a teacher and a specific child, or when the teacher is simply not good at her or his job. We expect that all teachers encounter children with whom they simply cannot form a positive relationship, that there are children who "push buttons" in ways the teacher cannot tolerate or rise above. In that case we would expect a teacher to be involved in a decision-making process with her or his supervisor that would not prolong that relationship past an initial year. In the case of the burned-out, inexperienced, or untrained teacher, we would expect that most of the children will be suffering in that classroom, and it remains a job for the administration to handle. But as our examples have illustrated, with care and attention to these more negative possibilities, the potential benefits of keeping children and teachers together are large.

COOPERATIVE LEARNING AND PEER TUTORING

The research on cooperative learning and on peer tutoring suggests that as well as having potential academic benefits, these classroom organizational forms are associated with increases in positive relationships and classroom climates (Battistich, Schaps, Watson, & Solumon, 1996).

In our observations, teachers who were successful at fostering positive child-teacher relationships and classroom climates conveyed the expectation that all the children as well as the teacher were responsible for everyone's learning. For example, Ms. Wallis has organized her kindergarten class so that groups of children have been assigned problems that require a group of children to work together. As the groups work, she moves among them, observing, listening, and at times intervening to extend their learning. In the following narrative, a group is to divide themselves so that some are entering data on the computer while others are coloring.

Ms. Wallis is roaming around the classroom seeing how the groups are doing. When she comes upon a group in which only Jason is coloring and doing all the computer work, she asks, "David, have you done any of the work?" David shakes his head. She points out, "Jason's doing two things, coloring and doing the computer work. You need to split it up so one person is coloring and one person is doing the computer things." David says, "OK, I'll color."

Because of the children's familiarity with cooperative learning, Ms. Wallis needed only to remind the children of their responsibility to share the work, and the boys readily agreed to work together.

In the narrative that follows, one first grader shares her excitement about making a connection between print and something that interests her. As a result, the children are companions in a learning process. Their ability to read is extended in a way that builds a close relationship.

Kameron and Brenna are sitting at the same table. Kameron is drawing in his journal, and Brenna is reading a book on whales. Brenna says, "Ooh! Look at this grey whale," and turns the book so Kameron can see. Kameron looks and smiles. Brenna goes back to her book and in a few minutes calls Kameron's attention to a blue whale. Kameron shows more interest this time and says, "I saw a blue whale at the museum. It took up the whole ceiling." Kameron returns to his journal, finishes what he has been working on, and shows it to his teacher. He then goes to the bookshelf, selects a book on marine mammals, and brings it back to the table. The two children compare the pictures in the two books and discuss whales.

In the next narrative, kindergartners have been asked to work in small groups to discover patterns. They are at an activity table piled with small wooden cubes, small blocks in many colors and shapes, plastic people, and beads of many shapes and sizes. By working together, alternating turns, Madelynne and Cristal solve a mathematics problem.

Madelynne picks an orange block and lays it on the table. She picks up several blocks of the same color and shape and starts to build a tower. Cristal comes over and they start to build together. They work collaboratively, taking turns. Cristal is using blue blocks, so an alternating pattern soon emerges. The orange and blue blocks are running out. Madelynne balances two yellow triangles and a small green block on top of a cylindrical red block. Cristal says, "It is going to fall." Madelynne demonstrates that if they are stacked just so, all will be well. The girls then turn to the plastic people and discuss what to do with them. They arrange them neatly on the structure in definite patterns as well as in color groups.

As these examples illustrate, there is great potential in cooperative learning for fostering positive relationships and learning. This classroom organization works well only when the teacher attends to patterns of interaction as well as to learning. Recall our earlier examples in Chapter 2 when conflictual interactions disrupted learning in groups.

SUMMARY

Having much the same effect as teacher behaviors that are consistently firm and positive, classroom organizations that are consistent and routinized appear to provide children with a framework for trusting the teacher. Many children coping with difficult life circumstances live disorganized lives—moving between foster care settings, being evicted or homeless, or not being able to predict the behavior of a mentally ill or erratic caregiver. We suspect that when child care or school provides an orderly structure—first there is free play and then there is snack and going outside—and when the same teacher and children are present over an extended time period, children can move toward trying out more trusting relationships. They can begin to relax their vigilance and preoccupation with anticipating and worrying about change and loss.

In our observations we also found that classrooms that included teachers who were fostering positive child-teacher relationships tended to promote relationships between and among peers by means of cooperative learning, peer tutoring, or both. By including the peer group as part of the learning process, teachers may be demonstrating that they value relationships.

Again a cautionary note: as in the preceding chapter when we pointed out that facilitative teacher behaviors occurred in the context of warm and positive classroom climates, we want to emphasize that the classroom organizations we identified were in the context of warm and responsive teachers.

III

The Teacher, the Child, and the Whole Classroom of Children: Creation and Preservation of the Community

Unlike the construction of child–mother attachment relationships, child–teacher relationships are constructed within classrooms in which there are usually many children and only one teacher. As we have discussed, children enter classrooms with fairly well-established, and often maladaptive, patterns of interacting with adults. As our narratives have illustrated, it often takes very little for children to move from productive learning to disruptive behavior. The task of the teacher in these situations is to simultaneously attend to the individual child and to the group of children. In Part II we discussed strategies that the successful teachers in our observations used to help individual children move toward trusting and secure child–teacher relationships. In Part III we will discuss strategies that teachers in our narrative studies used in order to involve the entire classroom in the process of constructing secure relationships and in creating a community in which all children can learn.

Chapter 7 concerns teacher behaviors and classroom organizations that enhance children's beliefs that school will be a safe place. This is particularly meaningful for children who face difficult life circumstances and are exposed to high levels of domestic and neighborhood violence. It also is important that the classroom be a safe place with regard to gender, race, sexual orientation, and other differences. We use our narratives to illustrate teacher strategies and classroom organizations that promote children's trust in the classroom as a safe place to participate and learn.

Chapter 8 focuses directly on peer relations. We review research on transitions in children's development of social competence with peers in order to build an argument for teacher responsibility for intervention in the process of developing peer social competence. We examine how teacher intervention at particular developmental transitions may enhance children's development. We then explore the evidence that peers may form a separate culture from one based on child–adult interaction. We examine the implications of peer socialization within a classroom.

In Chapter 9 we directly address the notion of classrooms as communities. In this section we use narrative analysis to illustrate and discuss strategies used by observed teachers to involve the entire classroom in the process of constructing secure relationships and pro-social communities.

7

Teacher Behaviors and Safe Classroom Climates

We have divided into two sections this chapter on creating classrooms that feel like safe places for children. The first section is based on teacher behaviors—how do teachers communicate to children that the classroom is a safe place? The second section is based on classroom climate—how do teachers help all the children create a classroom in which everyone contributes to making it safe?

We need to begin by discussing what we mean by *safe*. This leads us to issues of race, language, gender, and family configuration. Children coping with difficult life circumstances, as well as many children in our urban centers, are likely to attend child-care programs and elementary schools in which most families do not belong to the dominant culture. Child-care teachers are more likely than elementary teachers to be similar to these children in race, culture, and home language, teachers in elementary schools being more frequently from the dominant culture. But regardless of the personal characteristics of the teacher, schools and most child-care programs are based on a model of school success that is defined by the majority culture. The home culture experienced by the children may or may not share this model of school success.

Discontinuity between home and school culture may make it difficult for children to feel safe in school (Baker, Terry, Bridger, & Winsor, 1997; Wang & Gordon, 1994). Instead of feeling safe, children may feel out of place, unwanted, or unsure about how to behave and whom to trust. Positive, trusting relationships within school help bridge the discontinuity (Baker, 1996).

A powerful argument for making such a bridge is that it enables children who come from a home culture that is different from the school culture to gain access to the culture of school. Children who have access to the culture of school as opposed to being excluded from it are able to develop the competencies that support school success as defined by the school (Baker et al., 1997; Wang & Gordon, 1994).

In order for children to feel safe in school when they come from a different cultural context, they must trust that they will not be shamed because of differences in their race, ethnicity, or language. In the following two narratives, White teachers appear to share a belief that the African American children in their class need to be aware that Standard English and Black English are not always the same. The two teachers handle the situation in very different ways.

> Tanya is an African American child in the second grade. She attends a school composed of about 40% African Americans, 50% Latinos, and 10% Whites. Her teacher is White. Tanya raises her hand to tell her teacher something she considers relevant to the conversation. "Ms. Barter, I be goin' to the market with my mother." Ms. Barter responds, her voice and manner impatient and irritated, "'I be goin', I be goin', I be goin' ' . . . NO, Tanya, I have told you all a million times, 'I am going, I am going.' Try it, Tanya, repeat after me 'I am going.'" Tanya meekly says, "I am going," and slides down into her seat.

Ms. Hudson teaches third grade in a school with similar demographics. She has given careful thought to her response to the use of Black English in her classroom. She has also deliberated on the use of Spanish in the class by her Latino students. She believes that children need to have access to the spoken and written language of the dominant culture. She feels that is the only way that the children in her classes will have a chance at higher education. She also deeply values the home culture of the children and has come to think that she must consistently validate it, while at the same time helping her students understand the power structure that in many ways dictates their lives and futures. At the beginning of the school year, she began having conversations with her students much like the one that follows.

> There are two sentences written on the blackboard:
>   1. I be goin to the basketball game today
>   2. I am going to the basketball game today.
> Ms. Hudson asks, "Which of these two is correct?" Hands wave in the air, children call out, "Number 2. Number 2." Ms. Hudson looks confused and says, "Number 1 is wrong? I know I heard Anthony tell Marcus that very thing just a few minutes ago; how can it be wrong?" La Toya raises her hand. "Yeah, but number 2 is the way in school." Ms. Hudson says, "Exactly, number 2 is the way in school, but does that make number 1 wrong?" The students look confused, and Ms. Hudson continues, "I hear you guys talking on the playground, and many of you speak quite differently outside than you do in here. Many of you speak in Spanish. Is that wrong?" The students shake their heads no. "Many of you speak in sentences like number 1 on the board. Is that wrong?" No one replies. Ms. Hudson says, "La Toya was right, number 2 is the

way we do it in school. Why do you suppose I am always correcting your grammar and the way you say and write things? It is not because what you say and write is wrong; it is because you need to learn both ways. If you know both ways then you can make decisions about which way you wish to speak and when. If you don't know both ways, then you don't have the choice."

We think that Ms. Hudson and Ms. Barter would agree that children must use Standard English if they are to succeed in school. The critical difference in these examples is that Ms. Hudson enacts this belief without shaming her students for their race or home language.

In addition to race and language being sources of bias, teacher and classmate behaviors that are disrespectful to gender and family configuration can make children who are different feel unsafe. For reasons that are different from and related to race and language, schools often do not feel like safe places for girls. A full discussion of the literature on silent and not-so-silent girls in school is beyond the scope of this book (Fordham, 1997; hooks, 1989; Howes-Mischel, 1999; Orenstein, 1995). It is important, however, to note that this literature suggests that race and gender interact so that both silent White girls and "loud" African American girls often feel that they cannot trust their teachers and classmates. It is counter to our goal of making the classroom a safe place for all children to accept the idea that nasty teasing based on gender is age appropriate. The name-calling and bullying that accompany it can have lasting negative consequences for children's feelings of social acceptance (Boulton, 1999; Kochender & Ladd, 1996; Sutton, Smith, & Swettenham, 1999).

Remember Danielle, from Chapter 2, who was teased by boys: "Aki yells at Danielle, 'Lilybodchik!'" According to our informant, Lilly, Danielle was teased daily for weeks because (we infer) she was larger than most of the girls. Danielle has developed resilient strategies to handle the teasing. "Rr, you're probably going to be my size when you get to high school."

We wonder how much damage was done to Danielle's feelings of social acceptability and her perception of whether she was a part of a classroom of learners, when she had to face the daily teasing about her gender and inappropriate (for a girl) size. We also wonder what Danielle's teacher observed of this behavior, whether she intervened, and if so, what form her intervention took.

Another way that young children can be made to feel different and less respected across gender, race, and home language and culture is through exclusion based on family configuration. Children who have lesbian or gay parents, children who are adopted, children who are in foster care, and children who live with grandparents or aunts may be left out if all the family stories inside the classroom are about traditional mommies and daddies. Far worse are the situations in which children or their parents are belittled or taunted for living in a family perceived as different. Again child-teacher relationships that help children organize their learning cannot be formed in this unsafe climate (Chang, 1993; Derman-Sparks, 1989; Ramsey, 1998).

> Several first-grade boys are playing soccer in the yard. The ball comes to James, who tries to kick it, but steps on it instead and falls on the ground. Alejandro comes toward him and says, "Gawd, you are so gay, you can't even kick the ball." He begins dancing around James saying, "Fag, gayboy fag." The other two boys join in. James tries to defend himself, saying, "I am not gay," but the other boys shout him down. There is a playground aide nearby, but she doesn't come over to help.

Back in the classroom, Ms. Waters has heard about the incident from some of the girls, who came in to report it. Ms. Waters has two concerns. She does not like the equating of James's less-than-competent physical behavior with being gay, and she is aware that there is a child in her class who has lesbian parents and she wonders how the constant slurs heard on the playground affect her. Ms. Waters has been unsure how to handle this situation. She has succeeded in reducing teasing and taunting within the classroom, but she knows that it is still pervasive on the yard. She has tried telling the children that it isn't nice, that name-calling isn't allowed, that it hurts people's feelings, but none of that has made a bit of difference. She does not want to make an issue over whether or not James is gay, but she does want to stop the homophobic comments.

> From her desk, she gets a picture book that talks about a family with two mommies being a normal family. When the children come in from the yard, she gathers them on the carpet and reads the book.

Homophobia is entangled with bullying in school playgrounds. Many adults hear the bullying remarks and want to jump in and say, "He (or she) is not gay." We argue, however, that such a response only gives the children the information that if he or she were gay it would be OK to taunt. By using a book that talks about a lesbian family as being just a regular family, Ms. Waters is working to disconnect being gay from being shamed.

HOW THE TEACHER CAN MAKE THE CLASSROOM
A SAFE OR SAFER PLACE

In each of the classrooms in our Children with Difficult Life Circumstances Study, we observed that the teachers explicitly told the children that the classroom was a safe place to be, and that the teacher would make sure that it stayed safe. The teachers in these exemplary classrooms followed through on this promise, intervening frequently to make sure the classroom was safe. One example of this type of reassurance was embedded in the long narrative in Ms. Accardian's classroom in Chapter 5. Although the main point of the narrative was to show how gathering information and problem solving was modeled, Ms. Accardian did not let Bob walk away when Juan was still upset. By doing this she reassured Juan that she could be trusted to pay attention to his feelings. A part of the narrative that we did not use earlier follows:

> Ms. Accardian continues, "Do you think we solved our problem? No, because Juan is still sad. We haven't solved our problem. So what would you do to solve it?"

Our analysis of the narratives from the Children with Difficult Life Circumstances Study resulted in three areas involving types of teacher behaviors that helped make classrooms safe: physical safety, guns, and addressing hurt feelings.

Starting with Physical Safety

All the classrooms we visited had explicit rules about hurting others, and teachers moved quickly to make sure that the rules were followed. As we saw earlier:

> In Ms. Rosen's classroom, Carolyn goes to push Henry. Ms. Rosen says, "There is no pushing," and holds Carolyn so that she cannot continue. Later that morning, Tim grabs at Carolyn. Ms. Rosen says, "No, Tim. Carolyn, I'll help him." and pulls Tim onto her lap.

Ms. Rosen clearly can be trusted to keep children safe from physical aggression. She does not permit Carolyn to push Henry, and she does not permit Tim to grab Carolyn. From these experiences Carolyn can trust that she will be helped not to physically aggress and that she will be protected from physical aggression.

> Mark and Abraham are playing with blocks on the rug. Mark moves quickly and knocks over part of the structure. Abraham becomes angry and throws a block, which hits Mark in the head. Ms. Miller exclaims, "What is happening here? There is NO throwing blocks." She quickly moves to see if Mark is OK. He is crying, but there are no marks. She comforts him until he is calm.

Abraham continues to be enraged by the loss of his structure. Ms. Miller says, "Abraham, you are done in the block area for today. There is no throwing blocks." Abraham is screaming and crying. Ms. Miller says, "I know you are really angry, but I cannot let you hurt other children. It isn't safe for children when you are throwing blocks." Abraham continues to tantrum for an extended period. Mark has returned to the blocks. Abraham says, "I want to play with Mark." Ms. Miller says, "I know you do, but you are done with blocks for today."

Teachers cannot be everywhere at once. Mark did get physically hurt. Ms. Miller must make sure that Mark gets enough attention to be sure that he does not need medical attention, that his feelings are acknowledged, and that he is comforted. She must simultaneously help Abraham to refocus on his aggressive action and its consequences, as well as acknowledge his anger at the loss of his block structure. She must balance helping Abraham to learn control with making sure that he is not shamed for his actions.

Another type of explicit discussion that serves to reassure children that the teacher will keep them safe in the classroom took place in Ms. Accardian's classroom in the fall. Although the instruction addresses not hurting other children because bodies are out of control, the context of the first narrative, immediately following an earthquake drill, suggests that larger issues of trusting the teacher to keep them safe are involved.

The children are settling into circle after cleanup time. Amy and Jill are pushing at each other, trying to sit in the same place in the circle. Amy says, "I wanna sit there." Jill pushes slightly against Amy so Amy is not quite so close and yells, "No!" Amy yells back, "Yes!" Jill even more loudly yells, "No!" Ms. Accardian tells all the children in the classroom to leave the circle then come back and sit down quietly and safely.

No one is getting hurt when Jill and Amy push at each other, so Ms. Accardian's stopping of all learning activity may seem extreme. Her behavior, however, calls attention to her insistence that all children are to be safe in the classroom.

A week later many children are pushing, shoving, and making noise as Ms. Accardian attempts to start circle. Ms. Accardian goes to the light switch, turns the lights off, goes to her place, and says, "This is not OK. This is not safe. I want you all to get up, move around the room, and when I call you to come back I want everyone to come safely, ever so safely." The children comply and when all have returned and are sitting quietly, Ms. Accardian says, "Now, I see people are being safe. That's why we are doing this. So people can be safe."

Concerns for children's physical safety extend into the elementary school years. The following narrative was collected in a second-grade physical education class.

> All the students are sitting on the gym floor waiting for Ms. Kent to give instructions for using the balance beam. She shows them how to get on it and what to do. All the students are sitting on the floor watching. Ms. Kent tells the students that if they are scared of falling or scared of heights, they do not have to get on the high balance beam.

Both Ms. Accardian and Ms. Kent are proactive around safety issues. With large numbers of children to keep safe, they are attempting to minimize incidents when children feel unsafe or could be injured.

When Guns Come into the Classroom

For children coping with difficult life circumstances, family and neighborhood violence is often a salient part of life. In our classroom observations real guns did not come into the classroom, but guns were a recurrent part of classroom dialogue. Children talked with their teachers about seeing guns and being afraid of guns. Gun play often became part of children's fantasy play. All the teachers we observed struggled with the issue of make-believe guns. We offer the following narrative not because we believe that forbidding all gun play in the classroom is the perfect solution for all children and all classrooms, but because it illustrates one way in which teachers worked to reassure children that the classroom could be trusted to be a safe place. In Ms. Garcia's preschool classroom, all replica guns, including those made by the children, are forbidden. Julio, a new child who has witnessed both family and neighborhood violence, is having a very hard time with this rule.

> At the rug where Legos are available. Julio makes a gun and points it at the other children. Ms. Garcia says, "Ouch! That hurts. I don't like it." Julio persists in pointing his gun at others, saying, "Pow-pow-pow." Ms. Garcia says, "You know what, you cannot shoot at my friends. We are going to have to take the gun apart." Julio "shoots" again. Ms. Garcia says, "No, we are not going to make guns, because when you make guns, they scare people." She takes the "gun" and disassembles it.
> At circle time that same morning, Ms. Garcia asks, "Why do we have the rule about no guns?" Sara, who has been in the classroom for more than a year, says, "Guns scare me. When I see children in this room playing with guns, I get scared." Ms. Garcia goes on to explain that guns are never safe, that guns hurt people very badly, and that if any of the children were to find

a gun at home, it is important never to touch it. Several of the children become quite animated and involved in the discussion of whether a gun could ever be safe.

Ms. Garcia accomplished at least two things by introducing a conversation about guns at circle time. She told the children that they would be safe from guns at school and she gave them some information about gun safety outside school.

In a first-grade classroom Ms. Lowell is introducing math manipulatives (small pieces of plastic that can be hooked together). She states a classroom rule and provides reasons why gun play is not allowed in her room.

"In our classroom it is not OK to make guns, even in play." She makes a toy gun out of the colorful cubes. "It is not OK, even in play, to make a gun, because when you pretend to shoot, pew, pew, pew, you are pretending to kill someone." She dismantles the gun.

Guns were all too real in the lives of the children in the Children with Difficult Life Circumstances Study. Their teachers made children's fears and experiences with guns a topic of conversation, and in doing so helped children feel safe.

Hurt Feelings and Keeping Safe

A recent large-scale study of kindergarten children suggests that for many children, early school experiences include being a victim of hurtful actions from peers in school (Kochender & Ladd, 1996). Two hundred children were individually asked if anyone in their class had (a) picked on you at school; (b) hit you at school; (c) said mean things to you at school; or (d) said bad things about you to other children at school. Almost one quarter (23%) of the children reported that they had had one or more of these experiences "a lot." The children who were most likely to report these experiences were observed to be the least likely to participate cooperatively in classroom activities and most likely to report that they are lonely at school and to wish that they did not have to come to school.

These and other kindergarten children reported different types of experiences of being the victim of aggression—physical and relational. Relational aggression "feels" different from physical aggression. Relational aggression is defined as involving hurtful, ostracizing words, as seen in such comments as "I'm not going to be your friend" and "Maria told me that Nancy is really mean"; and purposeful exclusion of children, as in "You can't play with us" and "Go away" (Crick, Casas, & Mosher, 1997; McNeilly-Chaque, Hart,

Robinson, Nelson, & Olsen, 1996). In the kindergarten study, children who experienced physical aggression were not necessarily the same children who experienced relational aggression (Kochender & Ladd, 1996). We might expect physical aggression to be the more serious form. Yet children who experienced more relational aggression in the fall of the kindergarten year were the most likely to express a dislike of school in the spring. We can infer that the kindergarten children who told interviewers that they did not like school, that they wished they did not have to go to school, and that they tried to find ways of not going to school did not feel safe in school. On the basis of our narratives and past research on school success and adjustment, we suspect that these children who did not like being in school were also not learning in school (Ladd, 1989).

It was the exceptional teacher in our more general observations who treated hurt feelings and relational aggression as seriously as potentially hurt bodies. For example, Ms. Ryan, in our study of children with difficult life circumstances moves quickly to disallow a fairly mild form of name-calling:

> In Ms. Ryan's class, Max says to Amy, "You're stupid." Ms. Ryan says, "There is no name-calling." Later that morning, Amy is playing with her lunch and says something about it being stupid. Ms. Ryan says, "There are no stupids at all."

In one of our narratives collected in a regular school classroom, a teacher and her students appear to perceive relational aggression to be the fault of the child being teased rather than a problem for the whole group. The teacher does not help the children view the situation from Jack's point of view.

> In a second-grade classroom, Ms. Loop tells her students about Jack, a boy from another class who gets teased about being a girl because of his longer hair. She says, "He went home upset, telling his mom that he didn't want to go to school again." Ms. Loop then has the students write advice to Jack's class. Ashley suggests, "He could find others who are being teased and make friends with them and he shouldn't say mean things because that will never help him make friends." Nancy says, "He should ignore those who call him names. When you feel good about yourself, you wouldn't care what others think." Ms. Loop nods approvingly.

In studies of preschool- and elementary-school-age children that compare children's reports, teacher's reports, and independent observer reports, teachers appear adept at identifying relational as well as physical aggression (McNeilly-Chaque et al., 1996; Rubin, Moller, & Emptage, 1987). It is interesting to note, however, that these studies find that teachers and boys are in better agreement about instances of physical aggression than are teachers and girls about relational aggression (McNeilly-Chaque et al., 1996). This suggests that girls' relational aggression is so embedded within the peer culture that unless a teacher is a good observer and listener, girls' difficulties are invisible.

Alternatively, teachers may not believe that they should intervene in relational aggression. They may believe that it is human nature to exclude and include. Or they may agree with Ms. Loop, in the preceding narrative, who appears to believe that it is more important to change the behavior of outsiders to make them more acceptable to insiders than to change the behavior of the group to include those who are outsiders.

"You Can't Say, You Can't Play" is an extremely sensitive ethnographic study that documents the experiences of one teacher's attempt to deal with relational aggression (Paley, 1992). Vivian Paley, a seasoned kindergarten teacher, announces that she is thinking about a new rule during circle time in her kindergarten class. The new rule will be "You can't say 'You can't play.'" The children are doubtful and loudly disapproving, arguing that their rules of playing depend on being able to say "You can't play." A few children, those most likely to be rejected, are hopeful.

It is noteworthy that throughout Paley's "story" the more dominant children, those more likely to say "You can't play" than to have the phrase directed at them, work hard to convince Paley that such a rule will not be workable. They argue that they are in charge of the play and to evoke the rule hurts them.

Paley enlists the whole school in her project. She attends class meetings in first through fifth grades. In each meeting she poses two questions "Is the new rule fair?" and "Can it work?" The discussions are passionate as children remember their own hurt feelings about being excluded. The older children encourage Paley to institute the rule because it is fair, because they feel bad about not being kinder to their classmates, because excluding certain people becomes a habit, and because little children have to trust their teachers to keep them safe.

So Paley introduces the new rule in the kindergarten class. When she implements it, she realizes that she must follow it as well. She can no longer forbid children to play in an area as a consequence of misbehavior. In addition, there can be no more time out—another form of exclusion. The children are pleased that the teacher will have to change as well. The rule is instituted with only minor mishaps. The sad children who were systematically excluded are happier. All the children are kinder to one another.

The kindergartners and the older children continue to work on understanding the rule. The older children introduce the idea that a classroom is a public place, not a private one. They want to know what the punishment is for breaking the rule. The kindergartners debate whether being mean is the same as not letting someone play, whether telling secrets is against the rule, whether talking about another child in a mean way is against the rule, and whether separate but equal opportunities for play are okay. But in the end, even the most resistant children find that they have fun playing with the children who were routinely excluded from play before the rule.

The evidence from this study supports our contention that by implementing a rule against exclusion, a teacher makes the classroom a safer place. It is clear that the classroom is safer for the excluded children, the outsiders who do not so easily fit into the dominant culture of the school.

The children from the dominant classroom culture, the bosses, as named by the second graders in Paley's study, were most resistant to a rule against exclusion. It was easier for them to unthinkingly and automatically continue to exclude the children who did not fit in than it was for them to intentionally include the usually excluded children. These dominant children were extremely articulate about their "right" to exclude those who were different. However, there is nothing in this account to indicate that by telling the dominant children that they may not exclude the outsiders, the classroom became an unsafe place for them. By making a rule for inclusion, all the children became safe and no one was left out.

Paley could have started the kindergarten year with the rule already firmly in place. But by engaging the children in the "talk" about the rule, she included them in the responsibility for the rule. This scenario is similar to those of the teachers we observed who moved from making the rules that keep children safe to including all the children in the task of making everyone feel safe.

INVOLVING THE CHILDREN IN MAINTAINING
A SAFE CLASSROOM CLIMATE

Once the teachers we observed in the Children with Difficult Life Circumstances Study had established that they were going to keep the classroom a safe place for children, they moved toward making all the children responsible for keeping the classroom a safe place. We interpreted their behaviors as expressing that the teacher *and the children* are both responsible for making the classroom a safe place. Earlier in the chapter, in a narrative from the fall, Ms. Accardian was demonstrating to the children that she was going to help them keep one another safe. In the following narratives from the spring, she asks that the children in the classroom take on this responsibility as well.

During cleanup, Juan calls Anthony stupid. Anthony runs to Ms. Accardian. "Juan said a bad word." Ms. Accardian responds, "Anthony, could you take care of Juan? Let him know it is not OK." Anthony turns to Juan and says, "Do not say stupid, Juan."

During another cleanup period, Ms. Accardian notices that Leslie is the only child cleaning up in the housekeeping area.

Ms. Accardian calls out to her, "Leslie, are you taking care of that area?" Leslie looks up and nods. When Leslie joins circle, Ms. Accardian says, "Leslie, can you let me know what is wrong with that area?" Leslie does not respond.

In the next part of the narative Ms. Accardian puts the responsibility for making a safe classroom climate on all the children, the ones included and the ones left out.

Ms. Accardian continues, now *addressing the entire group*, "OK, you know that there were four people working in the housekeeping area . . . Leslie, what did you want people to know?" Leslie, in a soft voice, says, "There were four people in the area and they were playing but, but, not putting it nice and neat." Ms. Accardian says, "They were just throwing things in there? But what are you trying to do right now?" Leslie says, "We are trying to clean up." Ms. Accardian says, "Thank you, Leslie. That was a very hard job and you know what I think, next time I'm gonna put you in charge of that area because I think you are really figuring out how to take care of it. So do you want help?" Leslie nods yes. Ms. Accardian says, "OK, you need to chose a helper."

To get to their bathroom, the children in Ms. Garcia's classroom must leave their classroom and walk across a courtyard that homeless people use as a waiting place. In order to keep the children safe, there are firm rules about who may open the classroom door and about staying together. In the following narrative, Ms. Garcia shares with Sara the responsibility of keeping the group safe.

Sara skips ahead of the group of children and a teacher going to the bathroom. She reaches up and is about to turn the doorknob. Ms. Garcia calls out, "Sara, wait for the teacher. It is not safe for all of us when you open the door." Sara stops. When the whole group is at the door, Ms. Garcia asks Sara, "What are the rules about the bathroom?" Sara replies, "Walk and no screaming." Ms. Garcia says, "Thank you, Sara."

When the teachers can move the sole responsibility for keeping safe from themselves to the group of children, they help children be part of a community whose members take care of one another. This is very respectful to the children; it says that they too are to be trusted. This shift from the teacher to the group is similar to the shift we discussed in Chapter 4 when teachers move from organizers to partners with children.

SUMMARY

As we analyzed the narratives from the classrooms that promoted positive child-teacher relationships and those that appeared to perpetuate conflictual relationships, we were amazed at the differences in classroom climate in regard to societal issues. Attachment theorists rarely consider larger issues of race, gender, and home language. Yet these societal divisions loom large in urban child-care centers and schools nested within diverse neighborhoods. Positive attachment relationships are built on trust or felt security. Children cannot trust when they are shamed for being different—in race, ethnicity, language, gender, or family configuration. We feel optimistic about society when we note the efforts of teachers to create anti-bias classrooms. As we have discussed in this chapter, the theme of being safe—from shame as well as from physical danger—was important in classrooms that fostered positive child-teacher relationships. To return to Baker's (1996) argument, positive child-teacher relationships can form a bridge to school success for children who do not belong to the dominant culture.

8

The Contribution of Peer Relations

Classroom climates are constructed by peers as well as by teachers. It is both peers and teachers who make classrooms safe or unsafe places for learning. In this chapter we will focus on peer relations, examining how they shape classroom climates and how classroom climates shape them. Although parents are important in children's development of social competence with peers (see, for example, Sroufe, Egeland, & Carlson, 1998), most children construct their peer relations within child-care and school classrooms.

Developmental and clinical psychologists have traditionally been more focused on peer relationships than have educational researchers. For those for whom this material is new, we begin with a description of social competence with peers, followed by an examination of developmental trends in peer relations. We then explore two relevant dimensions of influence on the development of social competence with peers: teachers and the social-emotional climate of the classrooms. Finally, we examine how the peer group itself becomes a source of socialization for peer relations (Coie, 1990; Howes, 1988; Ladd & Burgess, 1999) and for rules of conduct (Maccoby, 1998).

SOCIAL COMPETENCE WITH PEERS

Social competence in peer relations has two interdependent components: social-interaction skills and friendship. Friendships are essentially affective relationships. An affective relationship is one that includes feelings of affection, or what would be called love in child-adult relationships. Children's friendships provide the participants with companionship, help, support, and intimacy (Bukowski, Hoza, & Boivin, 1994; Furman & Buhrmeister, 1985; Howes, 1996). Friends such as Jossie and Marissa in the following narrative spend time together, use each other for social support, and engage in intimate self-disclosure.

Jossie and Marissa walk home from school together. They live in the same apartment building and are in the same second-grade classroom. Jossie's

116

grandmother works in the afternoons and evenings, so both of the children go to Marissa's house, where her mother runs a family child-care home. As they walk home, they talk over the day, comparing funny and not so funny stories. Jossie says, "Was Diana mean to you again at recess?" Marissa says, "Yes, she makes me so sad."

Competent social interaction is generally considered as getting along well with peers (Asher & Coie, 1990; Howes, 1988). Prosocial behavior—helping, sharing, and enhancing relationships with peers—and complex play are indicators of social competence (Hart, McGee, & Hernandez, 1993; Ladd & Price, 1993). The value of prosocial peer behaviors to classroom interactions are apparent in the next narrative.

The students have been asked to work in their morning work groups. The red group is assigned to complete a math page that requires the use of crayons. Cyd, Marcie, and Mark all begin working earnestly on their papers. Dylan is rooting around in his desk, looking for his crayons. Ms. Streak looks up and reminds Dylan to get to work quietly. Dylan looks upset and continues his search. Mark gets out of his seat and goes to Dylan. He taps him on the arm and quietly says, "Come over and use my crayons. I have lots." Dylan smiles and two boys begin working together.

Aggression and social withdrawal are maladaptive behaviors, indicating the absence of social competence (Ladd & Price, 1993; Rubin, Chen, McDougall, Bowker, & McKinnon, 1995). We have discussed at length the disruption of learning that happens when children are aggressive. Remember, as seen in the following narrative, aggression can be relational.

Emma, Myra, and Lani are practicing their dance routines on the playground. Myra is clearly in charge. She shows the two other girls what to do, and her ideas are the only ones that are acceptable. Lani and Emily both practice the moves that Myra has demonstrated. Myra says, "Lani, you are so good!" Myra whispers something in Lani's ear, and they both giggle and point at Emma and then dash off across the yard. Emma stares after them and then goes to a corner of the yard and sits there until the bell rings to end recess.

Social withdrawal, another form of maladaptive behavior with peers, means that children are not able to have opportunities to develop more complex social skills. All children need some time away from peers, especially when they are cared for in groups. Social withdrawal, however, is a persistent and marked avoidance of peers, such as Luke demonstrates in the following narrative.

The class is playing dodgeball. Luke gets hit by the ball and is out. He was clearly an easy target, and some boys call, "Easy out, easy out." Luke goes over to the fence and starts pacing up and down, looking out at the street. Several other children get hit as well and quickly line up, waiting for their turn to get back in the game. All the rest of the children play throughout the physical education period. No one invites Luke to come back into the game, and he continues to pace up and down.

Generally, but not always, children who have friends are socially competent, and children who are socially competent have friends. Some children withdraw from peers at school and do not appear socially competent, but have neighborhood friends. Some children appear to be popular but establish their dominance in school with physical or relational aggression and may not be truly socially competent.

DEVELOPMENTAL SEQUENCES IN PEER RELATIONS

A fundamental assumption underlying our understanding of how peer relations develop is that children develop social-interaction skills and construct social relationships within groups of children. Therefore, we cannot merely say that 2-year-old children behave with peers in one way, and 6-year-olds another. The social context of the group is essential to our understanding of development and individual differences. Likewise, social interactions and relationships among peers become the basis of peer-group social structure and in turn become the social context for further development. Through early developmental experiences with peers, children internalize representations of social relationships and social networks, which become their relationship history with peers and, we assume, influence their individual orientations to the social world when they are older children, adolescents, and adults.

Infants and Toddlers

Teachers of young children used to be taught that infants and toddlers did not form peer relations, that they could not share, would only engage in parallel play, and certainly did not form friendships (Howes & Tonyan, 1999). These ideas began to change as relatively large numbers of infants and toddlers began to be cared for in groups and their peer interactions and relationships were developed within long periods of "everyday life events" rather than within relatively brief "socialization experiences." Children in child-care centers were with their peers every day and stayed in child care from breakfast time, through nap, until the end of the day. It was soon clear to teachers and researchers that infants and toddlers were socially competent with peers. Their play was interesting and complex, and they preferred certain peers to others. Friendships began in the infant room and lasted for years (Howes & Tonyan, 1999).

Thirty years of careful observational research later, we understand that infant and toddler social interactive play becomes progressively more complex in structure. The primary task for these very young children is to understand the other potential social partner to be a social actor and that social actions between partners can be coordinated and communicated (Howes, 1983). When children reach these understandings, they can engage in complementary and reciprocal play. Specifically, each play partner's actions reverse the actions of the other. A child chases her partner, then is chased. One child peeks at her partner; the partner says boo and then peeks back (Howes & Matheson, 1992). Research in cognitive and communicative development suggests that the representational underpinnings of these understandings are present in children as young as the toddler developmental period (Howes, 1987). Naturalistic observations established that toddler-age children constructing their peer interactions within full-time child-care centers were indeed engaging in complementary and reciprocal play (Howes, 1980, 1988).

> Kate is in the sandbox with Sanders. They are standing near one another, looking at each other. Kate starts to run, Sanders follows her, and they both giggle. Kate ducks into the hole under the slide and peeks out at Sanders. Sanders runs up to the edge of where Kate is hiding and slowly puts her head into the hole. Kate reaches out toward her and laughs. Kate spills out and chases Sanders. Both children run around the yard three times and then collapse in a heap on the grass.

The next developmental step involves incorporating symbols into shared play. Children everywhere, including those spending their days in peer-group settings, first begin to use symbols or to play pretend alone or with a competent adult player (Howes, 1985), but symbolic play soon enters the realm of peer play. Pretend play with a partner requires both that the child manipulate symbolic transformations and communicate the resulting symbolic meaning to a partner.

We see the simplest form of social pretend play, called cooperative social pretend play, among toddlers in full-time child-care centers (Howes, Unger, & Seidner, 1989). Play partners integrate their pretend actions by using a familiar pretend theme or script such as a tea party or phone calls. Similar to complementary and reciprocal play, cooperative social pretend play requires that children reverse the actions of the other, but in this form of play the actions are symbolic. The actions of the children presuppose that each partner understands that each player may engage in the symbolic behaviors. The children are able to share understanding about the symbolic meaning of their play, but this is communicated through the implicit script of the play rather than through explicit talk about the play. Nonetheless, toddler-age children are beginning to understand the role of the partner in constructing social pretend sequences.

> Jason and Reggie run up to the wagons. Reggie is barking and wagging his bottom as if he had a tail. Jason says, "Get in the wagon, doggie." Reggie leaps in and continues barking and wagging. Jason says, "I am pulling you in my wagon. We'll get a bone."

Toddler interaction among typical children is remarkably conflict free. Although there are struggles over who will play with what toy, these toy struggles appear to be more about the children not knowing how to play together than truly aggressive (Brownell & Brown, 1992). Toddlers at times seem to operate on the principle that what is yours is mine and what is mine is mine. As we might expect, toddlers who are more sociable are involved in more object struggles. The more sociable toddlers are the children who enter the toddler games with enthusiasm and "need" to use the same toys as their peers. Longitudinal studies suggest that the majority of these more sociable toddlers become socially competent preschoolers and older children (Howes & Phillipsen, 1998).

Toddlers who do not engage with peers do not learn how to negotiate object struggles and other rough patches of peer interaction. Over time these less engaged children may become solitary or withdrawn (Howes & Phillipsen, 1998; Rubin et al., 1995). At the other end of the spectrum, a small proportion of toddlers appear to be hyperaggressive (Rubin, Hastings, Chen, Stewart, & McNichol, 1998). Without intervention these hyperaggressive toddlers go on to become disruptive older children (Howes & Phillipsen, 1998).

Preschool and school-age children with difficult life circumstances often act with peers as if they were toddlers, in that they do not know how to play with others. They do not know how to enter into play, they do not know the rules for games that are familiar to most children, they often insist on having their own way, and they often grab a toy from others because they did not know how to play with it until they saw it used by another.

Preschool Children

Despite the new skills incorporated into cooperative social pretend play, this form of play remains a pale imitation of the well-developed fantasy play of older children that we label complex social pretend play. Toddlers have only just begun to transform symbols, so their transformations are not fluid and may be only partially developed. By preschool age, children's symbolic, linguistic, and communicative development permits metacommunication about social pretend play. Children can plan and negotiate the sequences of symbolic actions with fluidity, modify the script as it progresses, and step out of the pretend frame to correct the actions or script (Howes & Matheson, 1992).

> Janine and Sherry are engrossed in their play in the block corner. "We are going camping, and pretend that there is a bear, and you are the baby in your pajamas." "And I climb out of the tent and try to give the bear a cookie."

In preschool and kindergarten classrooms that set aside space and time for pretend play, children negotiate complex scripts, develop roles, and test out their fantasies and fears. In the following scenario, 4-year-old Cassie plays a game that she regularly draws other children into. She is a foster child and has spent many hours in court hearings. These hearings are frightening to young children, who worry that no one will be there to take care of them.

> Cassie says to Josh, "Let's play court. I'll be the judge and you be the daddy." Josh says, "No, I was the daddy yesterday. I want to be the boy who gets to talk to the judge." Cassie says, "Okay little boy, what do you want to say to the judge?" Josh replies, "I want to go home and be with my mommy." Cassie says, "No, you can't do that. You have to do what I say. Now you go over there to your fake mom and be quiet right now!"

Toddlers tend to play only with their friends. Their social interactions are more fragile and more dependent on rituals and routines than the social interactions of preschoolers. But by preschool age, children can play with children whom they do not consider to be friends. Preschool-age children also begin to talk about friends and friendship relationships. This ability to communicate friendship status to another is a new skill and a new source of conflict and hurt feelings. Perhaps this skill develops because preschoolers are now able to communicate the meaning of the construct of friendship. They use the language of friendship to control access to play: "I'll be your friend if you let me play."

A skillful teacher can ascertain when peer language concerning friends and play becomes relational aggression. In most cases it is not relational aggression, because children are not really angry with each other. However, while preschool-age children are no longer dependent on rituals to sustain play, their play is still easily disrupted. For example, a pair of children may spend 10 minutes establishing the roles and scripts for a pretend play narrative.

"You be the lion and I'll be the little boy who finds you in the forest and then."

"No, I want to be a baby."

"OK, how about you be a baby lion, and I'll be the little boy who finds you in the forest and then."

"OK, and then when you take me home, you feed me with a bottle."

If a third child attempts to join the play, negotiations may have to start all over again and may not be successful. If the child attempting to enter the group is a friend, the other children appear more willing to undergo the negotiation process if the friend knows how the game is to be played (Howes, 1988). A child who is a friend might enter the play by saying, for example:

"Remember the time I was the baby lion and then I got to be a great big lion, and I roared but I didn't really hurt you. I'm going to be the daddy lion."

A child who is not a friend does not have the same experiential background to guide her or his access to play. Just as teachers of toddlers may have to help children understand sharing objects, preschool teachers may have to help children understand sharing a friend.

Kindergarten and Beyond

By the time typical children reach kindergarten, they have the cognitive and linguistic capacities to be talented at playing with peers and at making, keeping, and losing friends. Children who enter kindergarten socially competent with peers tend to adjust well to school and to continue to enjoy positive social relationships with peers (Howes & Phillipsen, 1998; Ladd, Kochenderfer, & Colemna, 1996).

Individual differences in children's acceptance and rejection by peers tend to solidify during the primary grades in school. Children who by third grade are well accepted by peers tend to remain well accepted, while children who are rejected tend to remain rejected (Coie, 1990). Many studies suggest that in general, children who are accepted by peers tend to be children who are easy to get along with, who work well in groups, and who are not aggressive (Coie, 1990). For rejected children the picture is not so clear. While rejected children do tend to be harder to get along with, more aggressive, and less socially skilled, being rejected may contribute to these behaviors (Coie , 1990; Coie et al., 1999). As we saw in the Paley study, being rejecting and excluding may become an automatic behavior. Children purposefully excluded once or twice may continue to be automatically excluded by the whole group even when the situation or the behaviors change.

Children may reject others on the basis of difference rather than disagree-ableness. In one study of a school that includes children from many different ethnic groups, children in third through sixth grade were more likely than younger children to reject children of racial groups different from theirs (Howes & Wu, 1990).

TEACHERS' COACHING IN THE DEVELOPMENT OF SOCIAL COMPETENCE WITH PEERS

As we noted in Chapter 3, children use their attachment relationship with their teacher to organize their relationships with peers. In addition, teachers can directly influence peer relationships by supervising children's encounters with peers and by coaching children about peer interaction and relationships (Mize, Ladd, & Price, 1986; Mize, Pettit, & Brown, 1995; Mize & Pettit, 1997). If classrooms are to be communities of participants bound together by positive peer relationships, children must be able to play and negotiate with peers without acrimony. Teacher coaching of peer relationships may not appear, at first glance, to be directly related to learning. But as we have seen, acrimonious peer interactions quickly disrupt learning. By setting a tone and by making the rules of conduct for classrooms, teachers organize the classroom social and emotional climate that provides the context for children's relationships with peers.

Coaching to Play Together

Effective teacher strategies for coaching peer interaction change as children develop greater social competence with peers. Teachers of toddlers and teachers of children who have not learned to play can help by providing them with a structure for peer play. One study of toddlers found that the children who were most socially competent with peers spent their time in child care engaged with both teachers and peers (Galluzzo, Matheson, Moore, & Howes, 1988). This suggests that very young children or children who have missed out on developing peer relations are most successful with peers when teachers are present and helping them play along.

Ms. Rosen, in the following narrative, is working with children coping with difficult life circumstances who have not learned to play together. Carolyn has particular trouble sharing her teacher with other children. While Ms. Rosen sits next to her, she plays quite happily in the dress-up area. Her pretend play involves the area being her house. Alan enters the dress-up area.

> Carolyn sputters in protest, "I want to . . . " and then grabs and hits Alan. Ms. Rosen holds Carolyn as she punches and yells. She says to Carolyn, "Could you just tell him?" She continues talking to Alan. "This is Carolyn's house, so you have to ask her. This is her game, so you have to ask her." Alan says, "I want to play. Can we play?" Carolyn shouts, "NO!" Alan goes into the house anyway. Carolyn yells, "Noooo!" Ms. Rosen, still holding Carolyn, says to Alan, "So, Alan come out of there." Alan comes out. Carolyn stops struggling and says, "Alan, you can play with me." Alan gets his dress-up outfit and comes into Carolyn's house.

Ms. Rosen appears to have decided that her most immediate goal is to coach Carolyn and Alan through what researchers call a peer-entry attempt, rather than deal with the hitting ("Could you just tell him?"). Peers are most likely to enter an ongoing play when they observe some conventions—for example, ask to play, hover around the edges until they get asked, or suggest a subservient or complementary role (the small dog). Ms. Rosen gives Alan an idea about how to enter play: "This is Carolyn's house so you have to ask her." The first attempt fails: "NO!" but a forced entry doesn't work either: "Noooo!" Once Carolyn appears to understand that she has a choice about playing with Alan, she decides it will be okay: "Alan, you can play with me."

In the next narrative two younger children attempt to share the sand-box toys. Their teacher, Olivia, guides them through the interaction.

> Hector and Kayla are in the sandbox. Kayla cries out. Olivia approaches and asks, "What's happening? What's happening?" Olivia reaches Hector and Kayla. Each of the children has a hand on a toy bucket and is tugging to get it. Olivia says, "Oh, you both want to play with the bucket. Here is another one. It's just the same color. Hector, why don't you have this one and, Kayla, you have the other one. Are you making a cake? Is it a big cake?" With each child now attached to a different bucket, the pair begin to pour sand onto a large mound. Olivia steps back and continues to monitor the play.

Once again this demonstrates the value of teacher observation, Olivia appears to have correctly assessed that the struggle is over possession of the toy, not over playing together. She both supplies the toy and provides a script for continuing collaborative play. While it was convenient to have two of the same toy, we believe that the critical piece of this narrative was that Olivia did not introduce the rules of sharing or of taking turns. Introducing rules of play to the fragile collaboration of toddlers often overwhelms them.

Coaching to Play Pretend

As we have discussed, sharing pretend is an important developmental step. It is a particularly difficult one for children who have trouble trusting others (Howes, Unger, & Matheson, 1992). It is easier to communicate your fantasies when you trust that the other will listen, attend, and join in your play. It is harder to do so when you experience teasing or disinterest. This is especially true when a fantasy is a way of expressing fears and difficulties. With trusted playmates, children use social pretend play to resolve their own fears and to build intimacy with friends by sharing fantasies and having them accepted (Howes et al., 1992).

As children learn to play pretend with one another, their teachers can provide them with structures for understanding friendship relations. This gives children a chance to work through the normal developmental sequences of first learning to play pretend, and then using pretend as a way to understand friendship relationships (Howes, 1988).

In the following narrative, Ms. Hardy is sitting with the children as they play pretend. The pretend involves danger and rescue. Ms. Hardy's presence in the play keeps it in the safe realm of pretend.

> Alan, Mario, and Russ are playing a fireman game. It has been established that there is a fire and that they must call the fireman. Alan is announcing these facts, and as he does so, his voice gets louder and he flings his body around. It appears that Alan may be moving out of the pretend game into an out-of-control hitting and screaming episode. Mario looks anxious and as if he is not sure if it is a game or not. Mario says, "Is someone hurt?" Ms. Hardy looks at Mario and says, "No, it is just a pretend fire in an oven." She continues, "Alan, let me get you a telephone so that you can take care of it." Russ decides to call 911. Alan acts out putting out the fire. Russ hands the phone to Alan, who says, "I need a police car real fast."

Notice that while Ms. Hardy is in the play she is not really playing a character. Her role is to provide suggestions within the play frame that contain the anxieties of the children.

Coaching to Understand Friendship, Inclusion, and Exclusion

After preschool-age and older children develop the capacity to play together, they begin to sort out whom they want to play with (Howes, 1988). The distinction between playmates—with whom you can negotiate sharing, work on a project, and have a social conversation—and friends—whom you can trust for support and intimacy—is a difficult one for young children (Howes, 1996).

The following two narratives illustrate children's concerns and lack of knowledge about friendship relationships. In both narratives the children are making a common developmental error of equating friendship with inclusion in the group. Children who are first learning to play with peers have trouble keeping the play activities going when more children join the play. Younger children seem to solve this problem by limiting access to play activities to children who are labeled as friends. For these children, playmates and friends are equivalent. Older children come to understand that people can be friends without always playing together and that playmates are different from friends. Children with little experience playing or who have prior experience with poor relationships with others often have trouble making this shift.

> Max says to Randy, "I'm your friend. I'm everyone's friend." Randy says to Kurt, "Are you my friend?" Kurt ignores Randy, who is constantly begging him to be his friend. Randy says to Max, "No, I'm only friends with . . . ," and lists off everyone except Max in the class. Max then lists off all the children in the class, including Randy, as his friends.

> Diego says to Sara, "Who will play with me?" Sara responds, "I'll play with you, I'll be your friend." Juan says to Sara, "I don't want to be your friend," and takes his train and moves away. Diego tells Sara, "We can be friends." Sara moves her train toward Diego.

Max, Randy, Diego, Juan, and Sara are acting out their lack of clarity about playmates and friends. It is doubly difficult when one word, *friend*, defines both types of relationships. We observed teachers who, in our opinion, added to the confusion by saying things such as, "We are all friends in Room 1." We think they really meant "Everyone may play with everyone else in Room 1." It takes a sensitive and observant teacher to help children learn about inclusion, playmates, and friends.

For children who have trouble trusting others, exclusion is particularly painful. Teachers can be explicitly disconfirming of the relation between friendship and exclusion. In the following narrative, Ms. Accardian talks with the group about how people can be friends and still do things with other people.

> Ms. Accardian is conducting circle time. As part of ongoing work on identifying feelings and using discussion to solve social problems, Ms. Accardian has asked children to describe their feelings. As this narrative begins, Mario is concluding a long monologue about feeling mad and gives the reason: "Because Ben is playing with me too much." Ms. Accardian says, "And is that

what you're feeling mad about—because he really likes to be with you?" Mario says, "Because, because he plays with me a lot and he doesn't let me play with Andy."

Ms. Accardian says, "You know what then, we have a problem. We need to take care of it." She turns to Mario and says, "Do you like playing with Ben sometimes?" Mario says, "Yes." Ms. Accardian says, "Let him know that. Say, 'You know what, Ben, I really like playing with you.' So he knows that information. And then you need to add to it, 'But Ben, sometimes I like to play with other people.'" Mario looks at Ben and says, "Ben, I really like playing with you, but I like playing with other people." He looks at Ms. Accardian.

Ms. Accardian is coaching Mario, giving him some words to help solve problems of inclusion and exclusions. But these words do not completely solve the hurt feeling invoked by the inclusion-exclusion problem:

Ben nods his head yes and says, "But I also like playing with Mario and also he is mean to me, sometimes."

So Ben's feelings are hurt because, we presume, he only understands that Mario sometimes does not want to play with him and says so. And the narrative began with Ms. Accardian validating Mario's anger that Ben will not let him play with Andy. It is hard for a teacher to help children with such complicated social and emotional situations. Ms. Accardian has begun the process by bringing up the discussion rather than just leaving it to the children to solve the problem on their own.

THE SOCIAL-EMOTIONAL CLIMATE OF THE CLASSROOM AND ITS EFFECT ON CHILDREN'S PEER RELATIONSHIPS

As we have illustrated in Part II, child-teacher relationships are constructed within the context of the classroom climate. The same is true for peer relationships. While teachers are important in organizing the classroom climate, they are not the only participants. Children vary in the level of prosocial and problematic behaviors they bring to the classroom. Moreover, wider school policies may constrict or expand teachers' ability to set rules of conduct (Pianta, 1998). The classroom climate includes the level of aggression and degree of other behavior problems in the group of children, the nature of child-teacher relationships, and the frequency and complexity of children's play with peers. Using this notion of classroom climate, we can describe early childhood classrooms on a continuum ranging from positive, prosocial environments characterized by close child-adult relationships, intricate pretend play scenarios, and little disruptive behavior to hostile environments characterized by conflictual child-teacher relationships, angry, disruptive children, and little constructive peer play.

Past research studies limited the exploration of classroom climate to understanding children's behavior problems, particularly aggression. Studies of school-age children suggest that the level of aggressive, disruptive behavior of individual children is influenced by the level of aggression and disruption of the group (Battistich, Solomon, Kim, & Watson, 1995; Dishion, Spracklen, Andrews, & Patterson, 1996). In one study, boys rated as highly aggressive in first grade and enrolled in first-grade classrooms with other highly aggressive children were more likely than other boys to be rated as highly aggressive in sixth grade (Kellam, Ling, Merisca, Brown, & Ialongo, 1998). Children with similar individual levels of aggression in first grade, but enrolled in classrooms with lower levels of aggression were less aggressive as sixth graders than were the first group of boys.

One of our recent studies measured classroom emotional climate, individual behavior problems, and child-teacher relationships in preschool and used these measures to predict behavior with peers in second grade (Howes, 2000). The findings suggest that considerable individual variation in children's social competence with peers as second graders can be understood by examining both their child-teacher relationships as 4-year-olds in child care, and the climate of their child-care classroom. When children, particularly boys, were enrolled in preschool classrooms characterized by conflictual social interactions and relationships, and were themselves high in behavior problems and participants in difficult relationships with their teachers, they were likely to be aggressive and disruptive with peers as second graders. Children enrolled in similar preschool classrooms, but with low levels of behavior problems themselves, were likely to withdraw from peers as second graders. In contrast, children who were enrolled in preschool classrooms with high levels of complex peer play and who had had positive child-teacher relationships as preschoolers were pro-social with peers as second graders.

PEER CULTURE, SOCIALIZATION, AND LEARNING IN SCHOOL

While we have argued that there are important links between child-adult relationships and peer interactions and relationships, peer groups also retain independence from the adult social world. For example, it is rare for toddlers to engage with peers in the absence of adults. Yet toddlers in classroom settings invariably develop shared games and meanings that are autonomous from the adult social world (Brenner & Mueller, 1982). It is typical in toddler classrooms for the children to pound their fists and hands on the table in a rhythmic fashion every day when they are gathered for snack. The teachers are generally less than thrilled with this new game and try to discourage it. Yet daily, one child catches the eye of another, smiles, and hits the table with her hand, and the game begins. Another example is familiar to anyone who must spend time in airports. A toddler can play the game of run-chase—two or more partners look, smile, run, turn, smile, laugh, run, turn, laugh, run—with anyone else of approximately the same size regardless of language. These shared meanings are primitive forms of jump rope and other playground call-and-response games that are passed down among generations of peers on playgrounds. Children, as many adults can remember, during a certain limited period in development, know the words and rules to these games and are sure that adults never taught them how to play.

In our previous work, we have argued that by midpreschool, some games that children play are not interesting to adults, even the most devoted (Howes et al., 1992). For example, most 3- and 4-year-old children prefer to play pretend with only peers. Children are better at negotiating roles and scripts with one another than with adults.

Child A: I'll be the mommy and you be the baby.
Child B: No, you be the mommy and I'll be the other mommy who comes to visit.
Child A: OK, then when you are visiting the baby gets snatched.
Child B: OK, and then the other mommy says, "Get the ambulance."

Adults who play a role in this game have certain responses. They may be stuck with a child boss, as in this example:

Child A: I'll be the mommy and you be the baby.
Adult A: OK.

This rather quickly ends the play, since about half of preschool pretend sequences are spent in negotiation (Howes et al., 1992).

Or if adults continue to play despite the child boss, the adults often turn the play into a teaching situation, as in this example:

Child A: I'll be the mommy and you be the baby.
Adult A: Is the mommy bigger than the baby?

This again stops the play and is not much fun. Or the adult still playing with a child boss takes over as a expert player:

Child A: I'll be the mommy and you be the baby.
    Adult A makes sounds and gestures like a baby's that are so realistic that the child plays a supporting role.

Another reason for the relative independence of the adult and peer social worlds within classrooms is that there are, in most cases, simply many
more peer social partners than there are teacher social partners. For every
teacher as a potential partner, most children in early childhood classrooms
have as many as 10 to 15 peers. Even gifted, dedicated teachers can engage
on a one-to-one basis with each child only several, not many, times a day.
The experience of teacher availability is different for boys and girls. By
toddlerhood and onward, boys are less oriented toward the world of adults,
spend more time with other boys, spend less time interacting with teachers,
and are less responsive to the reactions of teachers to their behaviors than
are girls (Maccoby, 1998).

Maccoby (1998) goes on to argue that in terms of rules of conduct specific to gender, the peer group is a more powerful socializing influence than
are adults, whether parents or teachers. She analyzes large bodies of biological, psychological, anthropological, and sociological evidence to conclude
that children, early on in development, separate into gender-segregated peer
groups. Within these groups, children develop the social behaviors and interaction styles specific to their gender.

We suspect that in terms of how learning is organized in the classroom,
a similar phenomena might be occurring. Rules of conduct concerning how
to competently explore the learning environment and how self-reliant to be,
may be socialized within peer groups. In some classrooms, the rules for group
work and cooperative learning activities seem to include learning as much
as possible, using and recognizing the particular skills of the members of the
group, and so forth. In other classrooms, the rules for group work and cooperative learning activities seem to include doing as little as possible and
relying on the perceived smart kid for all the answers. Similarly, peer-
socialized rules of conduct could be developed around how much, and how
to, involve the teacher in group learning activities.

Our review of the available evidence suggests that since individual child-
teacher relationships and the social-emotional climate of the classroom form
the context for peer socialization based on the organization of learning in
groups, teachers can indirectly influence the direction of the rules of conduct for learning activities. But the processes and mechanisms of these influences deserves further study.

SUMMARY

In this chapter we have enlarged our view of classrooms to include peers
as partners in interactions and relationships as well as adults. We began with
an overview of social competence and developmental sequences in peer rela-

tions. This description suggests that to become "good enough" participants in competent and positive peer social interaction and relationships, children have a great deal to learn in a relatively short time.

Although much of this learning to be a participant in the peer group occurs within the context of peers only, teachers can play a role in the development of social competence with peers. The effective teachers we observed did not appear to believe that "playing children are happy children and can be ignored." We noticed instead that these effective teachers stayed with peer play, coaching children and contributing to constructing a positive classroom climate.

In the last section of this chapter we explore more fully the notion that peers may form a semi-independent culture within classrooms. There are some meanings (e.g., games like jump rope rhymes) that appear to be learned and shared within the peer group but not learned from or shared with the teachers. We suggest that rules of conduct pertaining to learning might also be socialized within peer groups.

9

Classrooms as Communities

Throughout this volume we have written rather loosely about classrooms as communities. The language of education offers many varieties of community: communities of learners (Lave, 1996); communities of practice (Rogoff et al., 1996); and caring communities (Baker et al., 1997). In addition, classroom management is being reconstructed by some teacher trainers as community building (e.g., Anderson, 1998; Kohn, 1996). It is therefore with considerable trepidation that we introduced the term *community* in this book. We are particularly cautious because each of these writings about community comes from a different theoretical tradition and has generated its own empirical research. However, we believe that the authors of these current works on community and others who focus on the importance of relationships, including Pianta (1998), are examining an approach to teaching and learning that is distinctly different from previous models and that our work falls within this large category of approaches.

Previous models of teaching and learning, in Rogoff's words, are one-sided (Rogoff et al., 1996). Looking at the extremes of these models, teaching and learning is either controlled by adults—the teacher is active and the learner is passive—or by children, whereby children construct knowledge and adult involvement is seen as a potential impediment to learning. In contrast, models of teaching and learning that focus on relationships and community are built on the understanding that all participants, both teachers and children, are active and have responsibility for creating a climate for learning.

We begin this chapter with a brief overview of theories of community and schooling. We then turn to our observational material to examine how teachers in our studies worked with children to create community.

WHAT DO WE MEAN BY COMMUNITY?

In our observational work in classrooms with teachers who are succeeding with children coping with difficult life circumstances, we found that teachers who are working to construct positive secure child-teacher attachment relationships are simultaneously working to construct a sense of community in their classrooms. Achieving a sense of community entails that children understand that they are part of a larger group and that being thoughtful and cooperative with others benefits both themselves and the entire group. Teachers in these classrooms expect that children will be sensitive and responsive to one another, just as the teachers are sensitive and responsive to the children. The teachers communicate that the group is more than a collection of individual children; that individuals matter, but the group matters just as much as the individuals. These present high expectations for children, particularly children with difficult life circumstances and prior maladaptive attachment relationships. However, there is some good support for these expectations. As we have discussed throughout this book, as teachers and children are able to construct secure attachment relationships, children become more pro-social in their peer relationships. Furthermore, other children in their classrooms rate children with secure attachment organizations as higher in leadership (Sroufe, 1983). So children themselves perceive children who have secure attachment organizations with adults as worth looking to for guidance and support.

Our theory of community is not a theory of learning per se. Rather, we propose a sequential model regarding relationships, community, and learning. We suggest that children who can trust the teacher to keep them safe physically and emotionally will use the teacher to organize their learning. We further argue that when all relationships within the classroom, including peer relationships, are positive, learning for all is enhanced. This is theoretically similar to Pianta's (1998) conceptions of the role of child-teacher relationships in children's learning. When relationships are positive, learning can occur. This similarity is not surprising, as Pianta also works from a formulation based on attachment theory.

Pianta's implicit notion of community differs somewhat from ours. He is more concerned than are we with examining a system of relationships that extends far beyond the doorway of the classrooms. He writes of teachers' relationships within the school, of school psychologists' relationships with teachers and with one another and with other school personnel. He also is concerned with relationships embedded within different institutions (e.g., how the nature and quality of relationships between preschool teachers and kindergarten teachers enhance or make more difficult children's transition into kindergarten). We agree that these are important areas to understand and to study. It would be naive to argue that relationships within the classroom are not embedded in a larger social-emotional climate and context or that classrooms are independent of their own wider social contexts of class, gender, and race. However, we have limited ourselves in this book to discussing relationships within the classroom, and those outside the classroom only enter our story as the "ghosts" implied in prior relationship histories and the biases from the larger society.

Baker (Baker et al., 1997), like Pianta, is writing for school psychologists. Again, we find many areas of agreement even though our theoretical traditions are different. Baker (1996, 1999; Baker et al., 1997) reminds us of the importance of the context of schools. She defines community as something beyond relational bonds between individuals and suggests that when there are positive emotional bonds, there are shared values, ideals, and goals. In caring-community schools, children (and, we assume, teachers) feel as if they belong to something larger than themselves and therefore are committed to learning as the school defines learning. She focuses on the children who fail to achieve this sense of belonging to the community and argues that if children do not feel that they belong they will be unable to act in normative ways at school

Baker's work makes a bridge to Deweyan ideas of democracy and character development because, as she argues, his ideas were rooted in relationships and oriented toward community (Dewey, 1916/1970). Character development or ethical development is central to another body of work allied with conceptually related approaches to classroom management (Anderson, 1998; Kohn, 1996). Kohn, and Anderson in her critique of Kohn, argue that when learning is organized in school to be adult run so that children are to be silent and teachers are to be in control, then children must be compliant and managed. They propose, as an alternative formation, ethical development, which has as a goal empathetic, transformulative problem solving. Within communities, in Kohn's definition of the term, children practice choice, autonomy, and self-discipline in both social and cognitive areas. He argues that activities such as class meetings and collaborative problem solving foster social and cognitive development, create caring relationships, and move children (and, we again assume, teachers) beyond discipline.

Kohn's argument is explicitly sequential. He argues that within a different type of learning environment, children build caring relationships that subsequently foster the intellectual and ethical development of individuals. Lave and Rogoff are the architects of the kind of learning community that Kohn argues promotes ethical development (Lave, 1988, 1996; Lave & Wenger, 1991; Rogoff, 1990; Rogoff et al., 1996). In a community of learners or a community of practice children are active in managing their own learning and collaborating with their peers. Teachers support children's learning through careful observation and attentiveness to their learning activities, providing some guidance toward the next step, and engaging in joint activities. Academic learning and cognitive development occur because children and adults learn how to coordinate with, support, and lead others to become responsible and organized in the management of their own learning and to build on their interests. From our perspective, Lave's and Rogoff's theories of learning cannot work unless positive relationships are built and trust is created. They perhaps would agree with Kohn that their model for teaching and learning within a community provides the context for the development of positive relationships.

In some ways this distinction of direction—does a learning community foster positive relationships or do positive relationships permit learning to take place?—is a very academic one. In practice, all these theorists and researchers would agree that both the construction of learning communities and the construction of positive relationships are important. Teachers often recognize that they must create both.

As a result of our observations of teachers in urban schools who were not part of our Children with Difficult Life Circumstances Study, we are concerned that some teachers who are attempting to construct a community of learners are paying too little attention to the construction of positive relationships. Too often these teachers conclude that they would like to build a community of learners, but the children are so out of control that they cannot.

We had the following conversation with a third-grade student teacher.

Teacher: So I set up this lesson on story and myth in Latino communities. I wanted the students to work together in small groups to discuss the story.

Response: Sounds like a great lesson to use with your predominantly Latino classroom.

Teacher: They couldn't do it. I had them fill out a work sheet on what they learned from the story instead.

Response: What happened?

Teacher: Julio refused to work with Maria. He wouldn't go over to his group. Then Sylvia said that Anna said that she wasn't her friend and burst into tears. By the time I finished talking with Julio and Sylvia, Tina and Hugo were fighting. I just gave up.

Until this episode occurred during student teaching, this teacher had argued that if teachers provided children with content that was respectful of their experiences, they would learn. We hope with time that this teacher will both continue to construct such interesting content *and* work to construct the kinds of child-teacher relationships that facilitate collaborative learning.

Our hope is that by focusing on the construction of relationships, teachers and children will be able to construct communities. It is important to help new teachers understand that they may need to try things many times and that there are many small steps and missteps along the road. Teachers, as they move from novice to expert, will hopefully find that their increased sophistication in teaching and understanding children and classrooms will increase their skill in effectively building relationships and ultimately community.

CREATING COMMUNITY

We analyzed the narratives from our study for practices used to construct community. We found several recurring themes—circle or story time, alternatives to time out, and children comforting peers.

Helping Children to Be Part of a Group in Circle Time

The current wisdom of early childhood educators in the United States holds that toddlers, and certainly not infants, cannot sustain circle time or story time. Yet we will begin this section with an observation of story time for infants. The observation was collected in a French crèche for children who are between 2.5 months and 3 years in age (Howes & Marx, 1992). French child care is conducted within a different set of expectations for children than is common in the United States. Whereas in the United States we value individual independence and achievement in our children, the French child-care teachers appeared to place a higher value on the creation of community—a group of children all responsible for one another.

As part of a study tour, Howes visited a regular community-based classroom that included 20 infants and toddlers. Fourteen of the children were 12 months and older. At story time all 14 children plus two adults cuddled into a tiny space—so that all 16 people were contained in a sort of a closet with three walls and an open end. A teacher sat at the open end of the collection of toddlers and sang songs and led finger plays for 10 minutes. The toddlers, each one with her or his body touching those of several other toddlers, participated with rapt attention. Not one wiggled out of control, cried, or "had to leave the circle." When story time was over, the toddlers tumbled out of the tiny space and continued their free play in the spacious classroom.

We are not suggesting that teachers of toddlers directly replicate this practice; we tell this story in the hope that teachers will think about ways to help our very youngest children feel part of a group.

One of the goals of circle time for children of all ages can be to create a literal and a symbolic sense of community. It can be an opportunity for children to recognize that they are all part of a group. The teachers in our Best Practices Project and Children with Difficult Life Circumstances Study were clear that circle time was a time to work together.

The children in Ms. Jones's preschool classroom are gathering for circle time. Sean takes off for the dress-up corner. Ms. Jones comes over to Sean. "You have to come over with the rest of the children." She picks him up and carries him. "I'm going to say you need to be with the group."

During circle time in Ms. Rosen's preschool classroom, Elissa is lying on the floor with her feet on the wall while the other children are singing a song. They make up the words for each verse about their "owees." Ms. Rosen says, "I'm going to help you Elissa. Yes, we're all sitting together."

With experience, being part of the group can become a positive experience for the children. As may be recalled from earlier discussion of this narrative, being part of the group is sufficiently important to Max that he gives up on having his preferred spot.

Max is attempting to join the circle, but he has selected a spot where there is no room for him. Ms. Hardy says, "Max, move over. There is no space." Max responds, "But I don't want to be . . . " Ms. Hardy says, "Well then, leave the rug." Max moves over. Ms. Hardy says, "Good, I'm glad you could find a space."

It was a quick decision for Max to make—whether to sit where he does not want to or to leave the group. This far into the year, the children in Ms. Hardy's class appear to believe that the group is important.

Alternatives to Time Out

Time out is used throughout the United States as a way to manage out-of-control children. As we illustrated in Chapter 7 with the Paley (1992) ethnography, it is an exclusionary practice—teachers say, "You can't play." Adults give children a time out by telling them to leave the group and remain isolated in a designated spot until some number of minutes have passed or until the child can perform some task—be calm, apologize, or say that they will not do whatever they did to cause the time out. We believe that this practice serves to disrupt rather than create community. Time out serves to cut children off from opportunities to practice, fail, try again, and practice some more their fledging skills at negotiating positive constructive relationships. Remember, when Paley realized that to be automatically inclusive rather than exclusive, there could be no time out.

But at times, children do need to calm down and to regain control of their emotions and capacity to regulate their emotions. As an alternative to time out, the teachers in the Children with Difficult Life Circumstances Study, particularly those in the therapeutic preschool, where most of the children were struggling with control issues, would remove children to the side of the group and stay with them until they had regained control. The following narrative illustrates this approach.

> The group is singing songs. Aaron starts to sing in a very loud voice, drowning out the others. Ms. Rosen says, "Aaron, that is too loud; please sing in a regular voice." Aaron continues to sing very loudly, and Ms. Rosen says again, "Aaron, can you stop by yourself, or do you need help?" Aaron continues, and Ms. Rosen scoops him up and takes him to the other side of the room. She sits with him on the floor, holding him on her lap. "I'm going to help you until you can sing in a regular voice. I don't want you to be away from the kids, but it is too loud right now." Aaron stops yelling and says, "I want to be with the group." Ms. Rosen says, "So, you're ready to sing in a regular voice?" Aaron nods, and they return to the group.

This kind of response can be made in ideal situations where there are two teachers, and where the children are small enough to be carried. It is more difficult, but not impossible, to ask children to be away from the group when there is not someone available to both monitor their behavior and assure them that their membership in the group is important.

> Angelo, a first grader, is sitting on the rug with the rest of the class. They are practicing their count-bys (counting by ones, twos, fives, and so forth). Angelo is fidgeting, and kicks his neighbor. Ms. Steep says to him, "Angelo, be careful of Carmen; sit Criss Cross Applesauce." Angelo ignores her, and the next kick appears purposeful. Ms. Steep says, "Angelo, you are having a hard time sitting with the group right now. It is important for everyone in here to learn. When I am worrying about kids getting hurt, then I cannot teach. Please sit at your desk and help us from there."

Ms. Steep could not leave the group herself. Notice her language as she asks Angelo to leave, her emphasis is on the group ("you are having a hard time sitting with the group right now"), not on Angelo's misbehavior ("Please sit at your desk and *help us* from there"). We watched Angelo sit quietly at his desk for 5 minutes and then also quietly join the group in a different spot on the rug.

Children Comforting Peers

Teachers are not the only classroom participants who are able to provide comfort to distressed children. Research suggests that children as young as toddlers are responsive to the distress of their peers (Eisenberg, Lennon, & Roth, 1983; Farver & Bransletter, 1994; Howes & Farver, 1987). Children in child-care centers in the United States stop their play when a peer cries, look at their peers and the teachers, go to the teacher for help, and provide comfort to the distressed peer. Children are more likely to respond to a crying peer if they have a reciprocated positive relationship with the peer (based on independent observers' assessments of relationships) (Farver & Bransletter, 1994; Howes & Farver, 1987).

Again turning to observations in France, children can provide comfort to peers, in the absence of teachers.

> One teacher is on the playground with 60 preschool children. She is alert and watchful, moving between groups of children, monitoring their activities. A second teacher is inside but near the door to help in emergencies. In my 30 minutes of watching I only saw two distressed children. One approached the teacher, who initially ignored the child then briefly redirected her to her peers. The second child spent 15 minutes crying as she was held and rocked by a peer. The teacher never approached her although she was within her line of vision. Eventually, the crying child was comforted and continued to play with her peers. (Howes & Marx, 1992, p. 363)

In one of the Best Practice Project sites, children are explicitly taught to provide comfort to their distressed peers. This is a program for teen mothers who are returning to school. These busy mothers often have missed chances to play, to be taken care of, and to be comforted in their own lives. The program helps them and their children start to provide care and comfort to each other. When a child is distressed, whether because of a "routine" bump, a misplaced lovey, or a misdirected action from another child, a teacher will go over to the child, place her or his arm around the child, and then ask all the children who are in proximity to help comfort the child. The teen mothers have the opportunity to witness many kinds of nurturance and care.

> Rosie and Tia are playing in the sandbox. Rosie gets up to leave the sandbox and trips, falling to the ground and scraping her knee. She wails loudly and her teacher Maria goes immediately to her. Tia has stopped playing and is watching with a very concerned look on her face. Maria is holding Rosie, but notices Tia as well, and says, "Look, look at this, Tia. Poor Rosie has hurt her knee. What can we do to help?" Tia comes over and kisses Rosie on the cheek.

The teachers in this program intend to help the children to understand that the responsibility to provide comfort belongs to everyone, not just to the teachers, and certainly not just to the child who accidentally (or on purpose) caused another child's distress.

WHEN TEACHERS STEP BACK AND WATCH

At times, teachers need to step back and just watch. Children need space and time to develop a sense of themselves as members of a group. In the following narrative, the teacher did have a hard task. There were two teachers and 10 toddlers in the classroom. Lunch was over. Each toddler had to have face and hands washed, have teeth brushed, be helped to progress just a bit in the toilet-training area, and be helped to settle down on her or his cot for a nap. It had been a busy morning, and everyone was tired. The teachers knew all too well what might happen if these exhausted children got "wound up" and overstimulated and were unable to drift off to sleep with a story, soft music, and a back rub.

> Jenny, Mary, Mercy, Justin, and Henry are in the toddler bathroom. This is one big room with five tiny toilets and five washbasins. Teacher Maria stands in the doorway. All the children are sitting on the toilets. Jenny begins to sing the "wheels on the bus" song. She sings in a quiet, almost dreamy voice. The other four children join in. Now all five are quietly singing. They are all relaxed. They are even skipping the finger and arm movements that they usually love. Teacher Maria watches with a half smile on her face. She is silent and still. After all six verses of the song, the children stop singing and quietly and calmly finish on the toilet, do their washing and brushing, and drift off to the nap room.

We suspect that if the teacher had either joined in the song or interrupted the singing to remind the children to move along and get ready for nap, this might not have gone so smoothly. But the teacher watched. She did not leave the room. She was ready to intervene if instead of spiraling toward relaxation and sleep, the children spiraled toward out-of-control activity.

Our second example is from a second-grade class.

> The children were given a "fair share" problem. They worked quietly at their desks trying to figure out how three kids could equally share nine cookies. After a few minutes, the teacher asked five children to come up to the board. Usually during this type of activity, the children would write out their strategies and then wait for their turn to present their ideas. This day turned out a little differently. Enrique wrote his strategy on the board and then looked over at his neighbor. Tina had done hers in a different way. Enrique said, "Wow, I never thought of it that way . . . tell me what you did." Tina began to explain the problem and Fiona chimed in, "Yes, I did that too." Soon, all the kids at the board were eagerly examining one another's work;

the kids at the desks were watching and listening. The teacher just stood back and watched.

Standing quietly and watching is very difficult for teachers. It takes rapt attention and trust on the part of the teachers that she or he has worked with this group of children long enough and well enough that they have a sense of community.

PRESERVATION OF THE COMMUNITY: DISRUPTION AND THE GROUP

Because the primary goal of the classroom is that all children are there to learn and because all children in the classroom must have the opportunity to learn, successful teachers balance the needs of individual children and the needs of the group. Teachers must simultaneously help children to learn that they are valued and that their behavior cannot interfere with the learning of all the children in the group. It is often difficult for novice teachers to attend to both the real needs of children who are expressing their hurt at an unfair world, and the learning needs of the classroom.

As the following narrative illustrates, one of the teachers we observed had difficulty with this balance. It appears that Ms. Garcia is so concerned that Joe have an opportunity to play out his feeling about a difficult life event that she ignores an opportunity to construct community in her classroom by guiding children in a shared pretend game.

> Ms. Garcia is sitting at a table on which are small blocks and replica people. Joe, who has spent the past few nights in a shelter because his family was evicted from their home, joins her. Joe makes a structure out of blocks. Ms. Garcia asks him if the people are scared when they have to sleep at the shelter. Joe says, "This is a jail, and this is the police." Joe continues to play jail. Amy and Eliza join Joe at the table and follow his play with interest. Amy takes a replica doll and moves it toward the jail. Joe does not protest. Ms. Garcia says, "Joe, you can tell the others not to play if you don't want them to." The other children move away.

Other teachers are clear and consistent in maintaining that being part of the classroom means adjusting their behavior to be part of the community.

> During circle time Carolyn is standing up, pulling up her dress. Ms. Rosen asks her, "Do you have to leave the rug?" Carolyn says, "No." Ms. Rosen continues, "Well then, sit down." Carolyn continues to stand. Ms. Rosen says,

"Well, if you can't do it, we're just going to go on." Carolyn continues to stand. Ms. Rosen says in a firm voice. "So, Carolyn, move off." Carolyn sits down, off the rug, but nearby. She quickly moves back to the rug, joining the group. Ms. Rosen says, "Thank you."

Ms. Rosen knows that if she engaged in a prolonged discussion with Carolyn she would lose the sense of the group that she was working to create during circle time.

It is the transition between cleanup and circle in Ms. Jones's classroom. Diego is lying on the floor. He has put the standing mirror on the floor with him and is playing with it. Ms. Jones says, "Diego, put the mirror away." Diego continues to play with the mirror. Ms. Jones continues, "So, Diego, I guess you don't want to do it." Diego ignores her. Ms. Jones says, "So, Diego, you can't stop then, right?" The other children have finished cleanup and are waiting for circle. Ms. Jones says, "We are ready. We are starting the music. The other children are ready."

Ms. Jones could have waited to do circle time until Diego was ready, but by doing so the entire group would have had to wait as well. She decides that at this moment it is more important to preserve the sense of the group than it is to work with Diego on cleaning up. She has decided that the group needs to be preserved.

COMMUNITY AS PART OF THE CURRICULUM

Teachers can work with children in classrooms, even classrooms of very young children, to help them view the world as a place that belongs to them and that can be bettered through their contributions. With the help of a skillful teacher, children can see that their "community" extends beyond the classroom, to the classrooms of other children, to the school yard, to the places where they live, and to places far away. Second graders can write books for kindergartners and join them for reading, third graders can write letters to the local newspaper to protest the closing of a park, and children of all ages can work together as in the following example.

Ms. Wong's second-grade class was consistently returning from recess unhappy about the name-calling and teasing that went on while they were out there. Some of the taunts were racist, some picked on physical characteristics such as short and fat, and all were hurtful. Ms. Wong listened to the complaints and the upsets and wondered aloud if there was something they might try to do to make the school yard a safer place for everyone. The children decided to make a book. Each child had a page on which she or he described and illustrated a problem in the yard. They talked about what had happened to them and how they felt about it. They worked hard to make sure that their printing was neat and the words were spelled correctly. Ms. Wong convinced the principal to let the children read some excerpts at an assembly and to pass out copies of their book to each classroom. Ms. Wong presented the book at a faculty meeting and asked teachers to rally around the cause as well.

The children tackled a task as a community. They identified a problem and worked to solve it together. They achieved results that motivated them to continue in their efforts to improve their school and went on from there to raise school awareness about trash in the yard and in the hallways.

SUMMARY

In this chapter we have attempted to make a bridge from our work based on an attachment theory perspective to that of other theorists and researchers working on relationships, classroom climate, and community. We suggest that there is commonality in our understandings in that classroom learning and conduct rest upon valuing social relationships. There is disagreement about directionality and focus. Our approach is that positive relationships are a first and necessary condition for learning.

We have extended a focus on a community of learners downward developmentally, suggesting that efforts to build community may begin in infant-toddler classrooms. We suggest that while there are a variety of strategies that teachers may use in creating community, at some point teachers need to step back and watch children create community themselves.

Throughout this book we have emphasized that individualized attention is important in constructing positive child-teacher relationships, but in this chapter we suggest that there needs to be a balance between the needs of the individual and the needs of the community. The effective teachers we observed moved consciously between working with individual children and working with the whole group. Again and again we watched them use every opportunity to bring the whole group together, even when focusing on one child, and to include individual children in groups.

Ending Thoughts

We began this book by posing a set of questions about teachers, children, and classrooms. We have used theory, empirical research, and narrative studies in urban classrooms to explore these questions. In our studies, we found many teachers who were deeply invested in constructing positive and secure relationships with children from difficult life circumstances. And we found classrooms where exciting learning was occurring for all participants. Now that we have described and analyzed the narratives and reviewed the research, we return to the questions that we framed in the Introduction.

What Kinds of Behaviors Do Children Coping with Difficult Life Circumstances Bring to Classrooms, and How Do These Behaviors Reflect Their Prior Relationship History?

Our theory and observations suggest that children whose life experiences lead them to mistrust that adults will keep them safe, physically and emotionally, enter classrooms with predictable patterns of interactive behaviors, which are based on their prior relationships with significant caretaking adults, including parents and teachers. From these prior relationships, children have obtained a working model of how others behave toward them and how lovable they themselves are. If these prior relationships have not left children believing that adults are secure bases and that they are loved and lovable, they will act in a manner that is disruptive to classroom learning.

Children with histories of insecure child-adult relationships tend to act toward new caretaking adults as if these adults can be expected to be angry, hostile, unresponsive, and inconsistent. Some of these children act in antisocial ways with teachers and classmates, and their aggressive, noncompliant behaviors can contribute to conflicts within the classroom, distracting themselves and classmates from learning. Other children avoid the teacher, and in their preoccupation withdraw from social or learning activities in the classroom. Still other children are indiscriminately friendly and overly dependent on the teacher. Again, their preoccupation with the teacher draws their attention away from developing self-reliant learning.

Large representative studies of preschool children's child-teacher relationships suggest that as many as 50–80% of children in child care have constructed insecure child-teacher attachment relationships (Howes & Ritchie, 1999). Studies of children from difficult life circumstances suggest that similar proportions of these children come to child care and school with insecure child-mother attachment relationships (Lyons-Ruth, 1996; Sroufe et al., 1990). This means that as child-care and early elementary school teachers start each year with a new group of children, most of the children have had at least one prior difficult relationship with an important adult caregiver. The implications of these statistics for teachers and classroom participants are staggering. It is no wonder that teachers again and again report that children come to school with patterns of behavior that interfere with positive interactions and learning.

How Can Teachers and Children Move from Conflicts to Positive, Mutually Reciprocal Interactions?

We suggest that teachers and children can move from conflicts to positive mutually reciprocal interactions by constructing secure child-teacher attachment relationships. Although the current "no-nonsense" climate of urban schools may lead teachers toward a didactic teaching of rules of conduct and a "zero tolerance" approach to misbehavior, our reading of the literature and our observations of teachers who were effective in creating harmonious classrooms that were conducive to learning point to a different approach. The bulk of this evidence suggests that only when children have internalized dispositions for regulation and control will classrooms become sufficiently harmonious for learning to occur.

Children develop these internalized dispositions for regulation and control through constructing positive child-teacher relationships and by having adults who validate and support their emotions. They are then ready to engage in positive reciprocal relationships and will be able, with their teachers and classmates, to cooperate in creating a classroom in which learning is not disrupted. Conflictual interactions are linked in this same body of evidence to insecure attachment relationships and to harsh and restrictive adult practices that deny or negate the emotional quality of children's experience.

How Can Understanding Children's Prior Experiences with Child-Adult Relationships Help Teachers to Construct New, Trusting Child-Adult Relationships?

Understanding that many children enter classrooms prepared not to trust the teacher and not to use her or him to guide their learning can be discouraging to teachers. We find encouragement and hope in the evidence that suggests that each teacher has the opportunity to construct new and different relationships with the children who enter her or his classroom. The quality of a child-teacher attachment relationship can be independent of the quality of children's prior relationship with parents and with previous teachers.

We believe that if teachers can see children's disruptive and provocative behavior as making both sense and no sense, they can begin the process of constructing different and more secure relationships. Children's disruptive and provocative behavior is sensible if they are acting as if adults cannot be trusted. Yet this behavior will make no sense if the teacher does not play her or his predicted part in the interaction. We suggest that teachers need to disconfirm these children's patterns of behavior by being unfailingly, perhaps boringly, consistently positive and firm. Over time the children notice that the teacher is not acting as expected and begin to change toward internalized trust and willingness to cooperate. In other words, children begin to cooperate because they are committed to a positive relationship with the teacher and because they trust that she or he will be warm, positive, and responsive.

While we have suggested that this pathway for teachers can be a successful and rewarding one, we do not mean to suggest that it is an easy one. To consistently disconfirm disruptive behaviors in a warm, positive, and firm manner requires a sophisticated level of self-reflective teaching. Teachers must be careful observers of children and willing to both individualize responses and constantly reevaluate and be open to changing their behaviors with children. We observe that teachers themselves need support from colleagues, mentors, and supervisors to follow this pathway with disruptive children.

What Teacher Behaviors and Classroom Organizations Are Associated with Positive Child-Teacher Relationships and Prosocial Classroom Environments for Children with Difficult Life Circumstances?

With observations and analysis of interactions between teachers and children from extremely difficult life circumstances, and our careful attention to interactions in many urban classrooms, we established that it is possible to disconfirm prior insecure relationship history and construct secure child-teacher relationships. We found classrooms that were exciting places in which to learn, where child-teacher and child-child interactions were harmonious and enhancing of individual and group learning.

A wide variety of teacher strategies and classroom organizations are described in this book. The particular strategies and organizations varied according to the developmental age of the children, their challenges and strengths, and the interest of the teachers. There are no magic answers in this tale. Instead we found consistency in the intent to establish positive class-room climates and communities of learners, and willingness on the part of the teacher to be "tough" enough to construct secure relationships with children. We hope that the descriptions of the practices will inspire others to follow in their footsteps.

How Do Teachers Balance the Needs of Individual Children and Still Construct a Mutually Responsive and Responsible Community in Which All Children Are Learning?

Teacher preparation in the United States tends to take an individualized approach. We suggest, however, that the effective teachers we observe constantly and successfully found a balance between the needs of individual children and the establishment of a community. Again we refer the reader to the wide variety of particular strategies and practices that teachers used to achieve this balance. We do want to emphasize that attachment theory is not a sufficient guide to practice in this area. Nor, do we believe, is sociocultural theory. Only when we move into the intersection between these two theories can we explore what it means in practice to walk that precarious line between the individual child and the community.

In summary, the children we observed are coping with poverty, homelessness, and disorganized lives outside child care or school. The strategies that permit them to survive these difficult life circumstances lead them to mistrust their teachers when they enter the worlds of child care and school. Their distrust is dysfunctional within school because it interferes with their learning and often the learning of the other children in their classrooms. Teachers may use knowledge of representations of child-adult relationships that children may bring to the classrooms to better understand children and support their learning. The effective teachers we observed illustrate how teachers can help the children in their classrooms to construct child-teacher relationships based on trust. These teachers then worked to create with the children communities based on mutual and reciprocal positive relationships. In these classrooms, learning was occurring. We are optimistic about the role of teachers in making a difference in the lives of children coping with difficult life circumstances.

References

Aber, L., & Allen, J. P. (1987). The effects of maltreatment on young children's socio-emotional development: An attachment perspective. *Developmental Psychology, 23*, 406–414.

Ainsworth, M. D. S., Blehar, M. C., Waters, E., & Wall, S. (1978). *Patterns of attachment: A psychological study of the Strange Situation*. Hillsdale, NJ: Erlbaum.

Alexander, K. L., Entwistle, D. R., & Thompson, M. S. (1987). School performance, status relations, and the structure of sentiment: Bring the teacher back in. *American Sociological Review, 52*, 665–682.

Anderson, D. (1998). Reconstructing discipline. *Journal of Applied Developmental Psychology, 19*, 659–662.

Anthony, E. J., & Cohler, B. J. (1987). *The invulnerable child*. New York: Guilford.

Asher, S. R., & Coie, J. (1990). *Peer rejection in childhood*. Cambridge: Cambridge University Press.

Baker, J. (1996). Are we missing the forest for the trees? Considering the social context of school violence. *Journal of School Psychology, 36*, 29–44.

Baker, J. A. (1999). Teacher-student interaction in urban at-risk classrooms: Differential behavior, relationship quality, and student satisfaction with school. *Elementary School Journal, 100*, 57–70.

Baker, J. A., Terry, T., Bridger, R., & Winsor, A. (1997). Schools as caring communities: A relational approach to school reform. *School Psychology Review, 26*, 576–588.

Bartlett, L., Goodman Turkanis, C., & Rogoff, B. (Eds.). (in press). *A learning community*. New York: Oxford University Press.

Battistich, V., Schaps, E., Watson, M., & Solumon, D. (1996). Preventative effects of the Child Development Project: Early findings from an ongoing multi-site demonstration trial. *Journal of Adolescent Research, 11*, 12–35.

Battistich, V., Solomon, D., Kim, D., & Watson, M. (1995). Schools as communities, poverty levels of student populations, and student's attitudes, motives, and performance: A multi-level analysis. *American Educational Research Journal, 32*, 627–658.

Baydar, N., & Brooks-Gunn, J. (1991). Effects of maternal employment and child care arrangements on preschoolers' cognitive and behavioral outcomes: Evidence from children of the national longitudinal survey of youth. *Developmental Psychology, 27*, 932–945.

Belsky, J., Garduque, I., & Hrnic, E. (1984). Assessing performance, competence, and executive capacity in infant play: Relations to home environment and security of attachment. *Developmental Psychology, 20*, 406–417.

Bergin, C., & Bergin, D.A. (1999). Classroom discipline that promotes self-control. *Journal of Applied Developmental Psychology, 35*, 189–206.

Berlin, L., & Cassidy, J. (1999). Relations among relationships: Contributions from attachment theory and research. In J. Cassidy & P. R. Shaver (Eds.), *Handbook of attachment theory and research* (pp. 688–712). New York: Guilford.

Birch, S. H., & Ladd, G. W. (1997). The child-teacher relationship and children's early school adjustment. *Journal of School Psychology, 35*, 61–79.

Boulton, M. (1999). Concurrent and longitudinal relations between children's playground behaviors and social preferences, victimization, and bullying. *Child Development, 70*, 944–954.

Bowlby, J. (1982). *Attachment and loss: Vol. 1. Attachment.* London: Hogarth.

Boyce, W. T., Frank, E., Jenson, P. S., Kessler, R. C., Nelson, C. A., Steinberg, L., and the Mac Arthur Network on Psychopathology and Development (1998). Social context in developmental psychopathology: Recommendations from the Mac Arthur Network on Psychopathology and Development. *Development and Psychopathology, 10*, 143–164.

Brenner, J., & Mueller, E. (1982). Shared meaning in boy toddler peer relations. *Child Development, 53*, 380–393.

Bretherton, I. (1985). Attachment theory: Retrospect and prospect. In I.^sBretherton & E. Waters (Eds.), Growing points of attachment theory and research (pp. 3–35). *Monographs of the Society for Research in Child Development, 50* (1–2, serial no. 209).

Bretherton, I. (1990). Open communication and internal working models: Their role in the development of attachment relationships. In R. A. Thompson (Ed.), *Nebraska Symposium on Motivation: Vol 36. Socioemotional development* (pp. 57–113). Lincoln: University of Nebraska Press.

Brownell, C., & Brown, E. (1992). Peers and play in infants and toddlers. In Van Hasselt & M. Herson (Eds.), *Handbook of social development* (pp. 183–200). New York: Plenum.

Bukowski, W. M., Hoza, B., & Boivin, M. (1994). Measuring friendship quality during pre- and early adolescence: The development and psychometric properties of the friendship qualities scale. *Journal of Social and Personal Relationships*, 471–484.

Canter, L. (1988). Assertive discipline and the search for the perfect classroom. *Young Children, 43*, 24.

Carlson, J. L., & Parke, R. D. (1996). Reciprocal negative affect in child-parent interaction and children's peer competency. *Child Development, 67*, 2217–2226.

Cassidy, J. (1994). Emotion regulation: Influences of attachment relationships. In N. Fox (Eds.), The development of emotion regulation: Biological and behavioral considerations. *Monographs of the Society for Research in Child Development, 59* (2–3, Serial No. 240). 228–249.

Cassidy, J., & Berlin, L. (1994). The insecure/ambivalent pattern of attachment: Theory and research. *Child Development, 65*, 971–991.

Chang, H. (1993). *Affirming children's roots*. San Francisco: California Tomorrow.

Cohn, D. A. (1990). Child-mother attachment of six-year-olds and social competence at school. *Child Development, 61*, 152–162.

Coie, J. D. (1990). Towards a theory of peer rejection. In S. R. Asher & J. D. Coie (Eds.), *Peer rejection in childhood* (pp. 17–59). New York: Cambridge University Press.

Coie, J. D., & Dodge, K. A. (1997). Aggression and antisocial behavior. In W. Damon (Editor in Chief), N. Eisenberg (Volume Editor), *Handbook of Child Psychology: Vol. 3. Social, Emotional, and Personality Development*. New York: John Wiley.

Coie, J. D., Dodge, K. A., Schwartz, D., Cillessen, A. H. N., Hubbard, J. A., Lemerise, E. A., & Bateman, H. (1999). It takes two to fight: A test of relational factors and a method for assessing aggressive dyads. *Developmental Psychology, 35*, 1179–1188.

Crick, N. R., Casas, J. F., & Mosher, M. (1997). Relational and overt aggression in preschool. *Developmental Psychology, 33*, 579–588.

Crockenberg, S., & Litman, C. (1990). Autonomy as competence in 2 year olds: Maternal correlates of child defiance, compliance, and self-assertion. *Developmental Psychology, 26*, 961–971.

DeKlyen, M., Biernbaum, M. A., Speltz, M., & Greenberg, M. (1998). Fathers and preschool behavior problems. *Developmental Psychology, 34*, 264–275.

Denham, S., & Holt, R. W. (1993). Preschoolers' likability as a cause or consequence of their social behavior. *Developmental Psychology, 29*, 271–275.

Derman-Sparks, L. (1989). *Antibias curriculum tools for empowering young people*. Washington, DC: National Association for the Education of Young Children.

Dewey, J. (1916/1970). Democracy and education. In S. Cahn (Ed.), *The philosophical foundations of education* (pp. 203–221). New York: Harper & Row.

Dishion, T., Spracklen, K., Andrews, D., & Patterson, G. (1996). Deviancy training in male adolescent friendships. *Behavior Therapy, 27*, 370–390.

Egeland, B., Carlson, E., & Sroufe, L. A. (1993). Resilience as a process. *Development and Psychopathology, 5*, 517–528.

Eisenberg, N., & Fabes, R. A. (1992). Emotion, regulation, and the development of social competence. In M. S. Clark (Ed.), *Emotion and social behavior* (Vol. 14, pp. 119–150). Newbury Park, CA: Sage.

Eisenberg, N., Fabes, R. A., & Murphy, B. C. (1996). Parent's reactions to children's negative emotions: Relations to children's social competence and comforting behaviors. *Child Development, 67*, 2227–2247.

Eisenberg, N. A., Fabes, R. A., Nyman, M., Bernzweig, J., & Pinneulas, A. (1994). The relations of emotionality and regulation to children's anger related reactions. *Child Development, 65*, 109–128.

Eisenberg, N. A., Fabes, R. A., Shepard, S. A., Guthrie, I. K., Murphy, B. C., & Reiser, M. (1999). Parental reactions to children's negative emotions: Longitudinal relations to quality of children's social functioning. *Child Development, 70*, 513–534.

Eisenberg, N., Lennon. R, & Roth, K. (1983). Prosocial development. *Developmental Psychology, 19*, 846–855.

Erickson, M. F., & Kurz-Riemer, K. (1999). *Infants, toddlers, and families: A framework for support and intervention*. New York: Guilford.

Fabes, R. A., Eisenberg, N., Jones, S., Smith, M., Guthrie, I., Poulin, R., Shepard, S., & Friedman, J. (1999). Regulation, emotionality, and preschoolers' socially competent peer interactions. *Child Development, 70*, 432–442.

Farver, J., & Bransletter, W. H. (1994). Preschoolers' prosocial responses to their peers' distress. *Developmental Psychology, 30*, 334–341.

Fordham, S. (1997). Those loud black girls: (Black) women, silence, and gender "Passing" in the academy. In M. Seller & L. Weis (Eds.), *Beyond Black and White: New Faces and Voices in U.S. Schools* (pp. 81–111). Albany: State University of New York Press.

Furman, W., & Buhrmeister, D. (1985). Children's perceptions of the personal relationships in their social networks. *Developmental Psychology, 21*, 1016–1024.

Galluzzo, D. C., Matheson, C. C., Moore, J. A., & Howes, C. (1988). Social orientation to adults and peers in infant child care. [Special issue on infant day care]. *Early Childhood Research Quarterly, 3*, 417–426.

Gartell, D. (1997). Beyond discipline to guidance. *Young Children, 52*, 34–42.

Goossen, F. A., & van IJzendoorn, M. H. (1990). Quality of infant's attachment to professional teachers: Relation to infant-parent attachment and daycare characteristics. *Child Development, 61*, 832–837.

Gottman, J., Katz, L. F., & Hooven, C. (1997). *Metacommunication: How families communicate emotionally*. Mahwah, NJ: Erlbaum.

Grant, J., Johnson, B., & Richardson, I. (1996). *The looping handbook: Teachers and children progressing together*. Peterborough, NH: Crystal Springs Books.

Grossman, K. E., Grossmann, K., & Zimmermann, P. (1999). A wider view of attachment and exploration. In J. Cassidy & P. R. Shaver (Eds.), *Handbook of attachment theory and research*. New York: Guilford (pp. 760–786).

Gunnar, M., Trout, K., de Haan, M., Pierce, S., & Stansbury, K. (1997). Temperament, social competence, and adrenocrortical activity in preschoolers. *Developmental Psychobiology, 31*, 65–85.

Hamre, B. K., & Pianta, R. C. (2002). Early child-teacher relationships and the trajectory of children's school outcomes through eighth grade. *Child Development, 70*, 625–638.

Harms, T., & Clifford, R. M. (1980). *Early childhood environmental rating scale*. New York: Teacher's College Press.

Hart, C. H., McGee, L., & Hernandez, S. (1993). Themes in the peer relations: Correspondence to playground interactions portrayed in children's literature. In C. H. Hart (Ed.), *Children on playgrounds: Research perspectives and applications* (pp. 371–415). Albany: SUNY Press.

Harwood, R. L., Miller, J. G., & Irizarry, N. L. (1995). *Culture and attachment: Perceptions of the child in context*. New York: Guilford.

hooks, b. (1989). *Talking back: Thinking feminist, thinking black*. Boston: South End Press.

Howes, C. (1980). Peer play scale as an index of complexity of peer interaction. *Developmental Psychology, 16*, 371–372.

Howes, C. (1983). Patterns of friendship. *Child Development, 54*, 1041–1053.

Howes, C. (1985). Sharing fantasy: Social pretend play in toddlers. *Child Development*, *56*, 1253–1258.

Howes, C. (1987). Social competence with peers in young children: Developmental sequences. *Developmental Review*, *7*, 252–272.

Howes, C. (1988). Peer interaction in young children. *Monograph of the Society for Research in Child Development*, #217 Vol. 53, No. 1.

Howes, C. (1996). The earliest friendships. In W. M. Bukowski, A. F. Newcomb, & W. W. Hartup (Eds.), *The company they keep: Friendships in childhood and adolescence* (pp. 66–86). New York: Cambridge.

Howes, C. (1999). Attachment relationships in the context of multiple caregivers. In J. Cassidy & P. R. Shaver (Eds.), *Handbook of attachment theory and research* (pp. 671–687). New York: Guilford.

Howes, C. (2000). Social-emotional classroom climate in child care child-teacher relationships and children's second grade peer relations. *Social Development*, *9*, 191–204.

Howes, C., & Aikins, J. (in press). Peer relations in the transition to adolescence. In H. W. Reese and R. Kail (Eds.), *Advances in child development and behavior*. New York: Academic.

Howes, C., & Farver, J. (1987). Toddler's responses to the distress of their peers. *Journal of Applied Developmental Psychology*, *8*, 441–452.

Howes, C., & Hamilton, C. E. (1992). Children's relationships with teachers: Mothers and child care teachers. *Child Development*, *63*, 859–878.

Howes, C., & Hamilton, C. E. (1993). The changing experience of child care: Changes in teachers and in child-teacher relationships and children's social competence with peers. *Early Childhood Research Quarterly*, *8*, 15–32.

Howes, C., Hamilton, C. E., & Phillipsen, L. C. (1998). Stability and continuity of child-caregiver and child-peer relationships. *Child Development*, *69*, 418–426.

Howes, C., & Matheson, C. C. (1992). Sequences in the development of competent play with peers: Social and social pretend play. *Developmental Psychology*, *28*, 961–974.

Howes, C., Matheson, C. C., & Hamilton, C. E. (1994). Maternal teacher and child care history correlates of children's relationships with peers. *Child Development*, *65*, 264.

Howes, C., & Marx, E. (1992). Raising questions about improving the quality of child care: Child care in the United States and France. *Early Childhood Research Quarterly*, *7*, 347–366.

Howes, C., & Phillipsen, L. C. (1998). Continuity in children's relations with peers. *Social Development*, *7*, 340–369.

Howes, C., Phillipsen, L., & Peisner-Feinberg, E. (2000). The consistency of child-teacher relationships between preschool and kindergarten. *Journal of School Psychology*, *38*(2), pp. 113–132.

Howes, C., & Oldham, E. (2001). Processes in the formation of attachment relationships with alternative caregivers. In A. Goncu & E. Klein (Eds.), *Children in play, story, and school*.

Howes, C., & Ritchie, S. (1998). Changes in child-teacher relationships in a therapeutic preschool program. *Early Education and Development*, *4*, 411–422.

Howes, C., & Ritchie, S. (1999). Attachment organizations in children with difficult life circumstances. *Developmental and Psychopathology, 11,* 254–268.

Howes, C., Rodning, C., Galluzzo, D. C., & Meyers, L. (1988). Attachment and child care: Relationships with mother and caregiver. [Special issue on infant day care]. *Early Childhood Research Quarterly, 36,* 403–441.

Howes, C., & Segal, J. (1993). Children's relationships with alternative caregivers: The special case of maltreated children removed from their homes. *Journal of Applied Developmental Psychology, 17,* 71–81.

Howes, C., & Smith, E. (1995a). Children and their child care teachers: Profiles of relationships. *Social Development, 4,* 44–61.

Howes, C., & Smith, E. (1995b). Relations among child care quality, teacher behavior, children's play activities, emotional security, and cognitive activity in child care. *Early Childhood Research Quarterly, 10,* 381–404.

Howes, C., & Stewart, P. (1987). Child's play with adults, toys, and peers: An examination of family and child care influences. *Developmental Psychology, 23,* 423–430.

Howes, C., & Tonyan, H. A. (1999). Peer relations. In C. Tamis-LeMonda & P. Balter (Eds.), *Child psychology: A handbook of contemporary issues* (pp. 143–157). Philadelphia, PA: Taylor & Francis.

Howes, C., & Tonyan, H. A. (2000). Links between adult and peer relations across four developmental periods. In K. A. Kerns, J. Contreras, & A. Neal-Barnett (Eds.), *Examining associations between child-parent and peer relationships* (pp. 85–114). New York: Greenwood.

Howes, C., Unger, O., & Seidner, L. (1989). Social pretend play in toddlers: Social pretend play forms and parallels with solitary pretense. *Child Development, 60,* 132.

Howes, C., with Unger, O. A., & Matheson, C. C. (1992). *The collaborative construction of pretend: Social pretend play functions.* New York: SUNY Press.

Howes, C., & Wu., F. (1990). Peer interactions and friendships in an ethnically diverse school setting. *Child Development, 61,* 537–541.

Howes-Mischel, R. (1999). *Why do all the girls have their hands down? Girl's silence in class and the promises of feminist pedagogy.* Unpublished manuscript, Swarthmore College.

Katz, L. G., & Chard, S. C. (1995). *Talks with teachers of young children.* Norwood, NJ: Ablex.

Kellam, S. G., Ling, X., Merisca, R., Brown, C. H., & Ialongo, N. (1998). The effect of the level of aggression in the first grade on the course and malleability of aggressive behavior into middle school. *Development and Psychopathology, 10,* 165–185.

Kobak, R. (1999). The emotional dynamics of disruptions in attachment relationships. In J. Cassidy & P. R. Shaver (Eds.), *Handbook of attachment theory and research* (pp. 21–43). New York: Guilford.

Kochanska, G. (1997). Mutually responsive orientation between mothers and their young children: Implications for early socialization. *Child Development, 68,* 94–112.

Kochanska, G., Aksan, N., & Koenig, A. L. (1995). A longitudinal study of the roots of preschool conscience: Committed compliance and emerging internalization. *Child Development*, 67, 490–507.

Kochanska, G., Murray, K., & Coy, K. C. (1997). Inhibitory control as a contributor in childhood. From toddler to early school age. *Child Development*, 68, 263–278.

Kochanska, G., Murray, K., Jacques, T. Y., Koenig, A. L., & Vandegeest, K. A. (1996). Inhibitory control in young children and its role in emerging internalization. *Child Development*, 67, 490–507.

Kochender, B. J., & Ladd, G. W. (1996). Peer victimization: Manifestations and relations to school adjustment in kindergarten. *Journal of School Psychology*, 34, 267–283.

Kohn, A. (1996). *Beyond discipline: From compliance to community*. Alexandria, VA: Association for Supervision and Curriculum Development.

Kontos, S., Howes, C., Galinsky, E., & Shin, M. (1994). *Quality in family child care and relative care*. New York: Teachers College Press.

Ladd, G. W. (1989). Children's social competence and social supports: Precursors of early school adjustment. In B. H. Schneider et al. (Eds.), *Social competence in developmental perspective*. Dordrecht: Kleuwer.

Ladd, G. W., & Burgess, K. B. (1999). Charting the relationship trajectories of aggressive, withdrawn, and aggressive/withdrawn children during early grade school. *Child Development*, 70, 910–929.

Ladd, G. W., Kochenderfer, B. J., & Colemna, C. C. (1996). Friendship quality as a predictor of young children's early school adjustment. *Child Development*, 67, 1103–1118.

Ladd, G. W., & Price, J. M. (1993). Play styles of peer-accepted and peer-rejected children on the playground. In C. Hart (Ed.), *Children on playgrounds: Research perspectives and implications* (pp. 130–161). Albany: State University of New York Press.

Laible, D. J., & Thompson, R. A. (1998). Attachment and emotional understanding in preschool children. *Developmental Psychology*, 34, 1038–1045.

Lave, J. (1988). *Cognition in practice*. New York: Cambridge University Press.

Lave, J. (1996). Teaching, as learning, in practice. *Mind, Culture, and Activity*, 3, 149–164.

Lave, J., & Wenger, E. (1991). *Situated learning: Legitimate peripheral participation*. New York: Cambridge.

Lewis, M., Feiring, C., McGuffog, C., & Jaskir, J. (1984). Predicting psychopathology in six-year-olds from early social relations. *Child Development*, 55, 123–136.

Lieberman, A., Weston, D. R., & Pawl, J. (1991). Preventive intervention and outcome with anxiously attached dyads. *Child Development*, 62, 199–201.

Lieberman, M., Doyle, A.-B., & Markiewicz, D. (1999). Developmental patterns in security of attachment to mother and father in late childhood and early adolescence: Associations with peer relations. *Child Development*, 70, 202–213.

Londerville, S., & Main, M. (1981). Security of attachment, compliance, and maternal training methods in the second year of life. *Developmental Psychology,*
17, 289–299.

Lyons-Ruth, K. (1996). Attachment relationships among children with aggressive
behavior problems: The role of disorganized early attachment patterns. *Jour-*
nal of Consulting and Clinical Psychology, 64, 64–73.

Maccoby, E. E. (1984). Socialization and developmental change. *Developmental*
Psychology, 55, 317–328.

Maccoby, E. E. (1998). *The two sexes: Growing up apart, coming together.* Cambridge, MA: Harvard University Press.

Maccoby, E. E., & Martin, J. (1986). Socialization in the context of the family: Child-
parent interaction. In E. M. Hetherington (Ed.), P. H. Mussen (Series Ed.),
Handbook of child psychology (pp. 1–101). New York: Wiley.

Main, M. (1983). Exploration, play, and cognitive functioning related to infant-
mother attachment. *Infant Behavior and Development, 6,* 167–174.

Main, M., & Solomon, J. (1990). Procedures for identifying infants as disorganized-
disoriented during the Ainsworth Strange Situation. In M. Greenberg, D. Cicchetti,
& E. M. Cummings (Eds.), *Attachment in the preschool years: Theory, research,*
and intervention (pp. 161–184). Chicago: University of Chicago Press.

Matas, L., Arend, R. A., & Sroufe, L. A. (1978). Continuity of adaptation in the
second year: The relationship between quality of attachment and later competence. *Child Development, 49,* 547–556.

McFadyen-Ketchum, S. A., Bates, J. E., Dodge, K. A., & Pettit, G. S. (1996). Patterns of change in early childhood aggressive-disruptive behavior: Gender differences in prediction from early coercive and affectionate mother-child interactions. *Child Development, 67,* 2417–2433.

McNeilly-Chaque, M. K., Hart, C. H., Robinson, C. C., Nelson, L. J., & Olsen,
S. F. (1996). Overt and relational aggression on the playground. *Journal of Re-*
search in Childhood Education, 11, 47–67.

Mitchell-Copeland, J., Denham, S., & DeMulder, E. (1997). Q-Sort assessment of
child-teacher attachment relationships and social competence in the preschool.
Early Education and Development, 8, 27–39.

Mize, J., Ladd, G. W., & Price, J. (1986). Promoting positive peer relations with
young children: Rationales and strategies. *Child Care Quarterly, 14,* 221–237.

Mize, J., Pettit, G. S., & Brown, E. G. (1995). Mothers' supervision of their children's
peer play: Relations with beliefs, perceptions, and knowledge. *Developmental*
Psychology, 31, 311–321.

Mize, J., & Pettit, G. (1997). Mothers' social coaching and mother-child relationship style and children's peer competence is the medium the message? *Child*
Development, 68, 312–332.

Orenstein, P. (1995). *School Girls: Young women, self-esteem, and the confidence*
gap. New York: Doubleday.

Paley, V. G. (1992). *You can't say, you can't play.* Cambridge: Harvard University Press.

Peisner-Feinberg, E., Burchinal, M., Clifford, R., Culkin, M., Howes, C., Kagan,
S. L. & Yazejian, N. (2001). The relation of preschool child care quality to

children's cognitive and social trajectories through second grade. *Child Development, 72,* 1534–1579.

Pianta, R. C. (1999). *Enhancing relationships between children and teachers.* Washington, DC: American Psychological Association.

Pianta, R. C., & Harbers, K. (1996). Observing mother and child behavior in a problem solving situation at school entry: Relations with academic achievement. *Journal of School Psychology, 34,* 307–322.

Pianta, R. C., Steinberg, M., & Rollins, K. (1997). The first two years of school: Child-teacher relationships and deflections in children's school adjustment. *Development and Psychopathology, 7,* 297–312.

Pianta, R. C., & Walsh, D. J. (1996). *High risk children in schools.* New York: Routledge.

Posada, G., Gao, Y., Wu, F., Posado, R., Tascon, M., Schoelmerich, A., Sagi, A., Kondo-Ikemura, K., Haaland, W., & Synnevaag, B. (1995). The secure-base phenomenon across cultures: Children's behavior, mothers preferences, and experts' concepts. In E. Waters, B. E. Vaughn, G. Posada, & K. Kendo-Ikemura (Eds.), Caregiving, cultural, and cognitive perspectives on secure-base behavior and working models: New growing points for attachment theory and research. *Monographs of the Society for Research in Child Development, 60* (2–3, Serial No. 244), 27–48.

Putallaz, M., & Sheppard, B. H. (1992). Conflict management and social competence. In C. U. Shantz & W. W. Hartup (Eds.), *Conflict in child and adolescent development* (330–355). Cambridge: Cambridge University Press.

Raikes, H. (1993). Relationship duration in infant care: Time with a high ability teacher and infant-teacher attachment. *Early Childhood Research Quarterly, 8,* 309–325.

Ramsey, P. (1998). *Teaching and learning in a diverse world: Multicultural education for young children* (2nd ed.). New York: Teachers College Press.

Renken, B., Egeland, B., Marvinney, D., Mangelsdorf, S., & Sroufe, L. A. (1989). Early childhood antecedents of aggression and passive-withdrawal in early elementary school. *Journal of Personality, 57,* 257–281.

Ritchie, S. (1995). *Attachment relationships of substance-exposed children with their caregivers and their teachers.* Unpublished dissertation, University of California at Los Angeles.

Rodning, C., Beckwith, L., & Howard, J. (1991). Quality of attachment and home environments in children prenatally exposed to PCP and cocaine. *Development and Psychopathology, 3,* 351–366.

Rogoff, B. (1990). *Apprenticeship in thinking: Cognitive development in social context.* New York: Oxford University Press.

Rogoff, B., Matusov, E., & White, C. (1996). Models of teaching and learning. In D. R. Olson & N. Torrance (Eds.), *The handbook of education and human development* (pp. 388–414). Oxford: Blackwell.

Rothbart, M. K., & Bates, J. E. (1998). Temperament. In N. A. Eisenberg (Ed.), W. Damon (Series Ed.), *Handbook of child psychology: Vol 3. Social, emotional, and personality development* (5th ed., pp. 105–176). New York: Wiley.

Rothbart, M. K., Ahadi, S. A., & Hershey, K. L. (1994). Temperament and social behavior in childhood. *Merrill Palmer Quarterly, 40,* 21–39.

Rubin, K. H., Bukowski, W., & Parker, J. (1998). Peer interaction, relationships, and groups. In N. A. Eisenberg (Ed.), W. Damon (Series Ed.), *Handbook of child psychology: Vol 3. Social, emotional, and personality development* (5th ed., pp. 207–289). New York: Wiley.

Rubin, K. H., Chen, X., McDougall, P., Bowker, A., & McKinnon, J. (1995). The Waterloo Longitudinal Project: Predicting internalizing and externalizing problems in adolescence. *Development and Psychopathology, 7,* 751–764.

Rubin, K. H., Coplan, R., Fox, N. A., & Calkins, S. (1995). Emotionality, emotion regulation, and preschoolers social adaptation. *Development and Psychopathology, 7,* 49–62.

Rubin, K. H., Hastings, P., Chen, X., Stewart, S., & McNichol, K. (1998). Interpersonal and maternal correlates of aggression, conflict, and externalizing problems in toddlers. *Child Development, 69,* 1614–1629.

Rubin, K., Moller, L., & Emptage, A. (1987). The preschool behavior questionnaire: A useful index of behavior problems in elementary school-age children? *Journal of Behavior Science, 19,* 86–100.

Rutter, M., Maughan, B., Mortimore, P., & Ousten, J. (1979). *Fifteen thousand hours: Secondary schools and their effects on children.* Cambridge: Harvard University Press.

Spieker, S. J., Larson, N. C., Lewis, S. M., Keller, T. E., & Gilchrist, L. (1999). Developmental trajectories of disruptive behavior problems in preschool children of adolescent mothers. *Child Development, 70,* 443–458.

Sroufe, L. A. (1983). Infant-caregiving attachment and patterns of maladaption in preschool: The roots of maladaption and competence. In M. Permutter (Ed.), *Minnesota symposium on child psychology* (Vol. 16, pp. 41–81). Hillsdale, NJ: Erlbaum.

Sroufe, L. A., Carlson, E., & Shulman, S. (1993). Individuals in relationships: Development from infancy through adolescence. In D. C. Funder, R. Parke, C. Tomlinson-Keesey, & K. Widaman (Eds.), *Studying lives through time: Approaches to personality and development* (pp. 315–342). Washington, DC: American Psychological Association.

Sroufe, L. A., Egeland, B., & Carlson, E. A. (1998). One social world: The integrated development of child-parent and peer relationships. In A. Collins & B. Laursen (Eds.), *Relationship as developmental contexts.* Hillsdale, NJ: Erlbaum.

Sroufe, L. A., Egeland, B., & Kreutzer, T. (1990). The fate of early experience following developmental change: Longitudinal approaches to individual adaptation in childhood. *Child Development, 61,* 1363–1373.

Stipek, D., Feiler, R., Daniels, D., & Milburn, S. (1995). Effects of different instructional approaches on young children's achievement and motivation. *Child Development, 66,* 209–223.

Suess, G., Grossmann, K. E., & Sroufe, L. A. (1992). Effects of infant attachment to mother and father on quality of adaptation in preschool: From dyadic to individual organizations of self. *International Journal of Behavioral Development, 15,* 43–65.

Sutton, J., Smith, P. K., & Swettenham, J. (1999). Bullying and "Theory of mind": A critique of the "social skills deficit" view of anti-social behavior. *Social Development*, *8*, 117–127

Urban, J., Carlson, E., Egeland, B., & Sroufe, L. A. (1991). Patterns of adaptation across childhood. *Development and Psychopathology*, *3*, 445–460.

van IJzendoorn, M. H., Juffer, F., & Duyvesteyn, M. (1995). Breaking the intergenerational cycle of insecure attachments: A review of attachment-based interventions on maternal sensitivity and infant security. *Journal of Child Psychology and Psychiatry*, *36*, 225–248.

van IJzendoorn, M., Sagi, A., & Lambermon, M. W. E. (1992). The multiple caregiver paradox: Data from Holland and Israel. In R. C. Pianta (Ed.), *Beyond the parent: The role of other adults in children's lives* (pp. 5–24). San Francisco: Jossey Bass.

van IJzendoorn, M. H., & Sagi, A. (1999). Cross-cultural patterns of attachment: Universal and contextual dimensions. In J. Cassidy & P. R. Shaver (Ed.), *Handbook of Attachment*. New York: Guilford (pp. 713–734).

Wang, M. C., & Gordon, E. W. (1994). *Educational resilience in inner-city America: Challenges and prospects*. Hillsdale, NJ: Erlbaum.

Waters, E. (1990). *Attachment Q set*. Unpublished paper, State University of New York, Stony Brook.

Werner, E. E. (1993). Risk, resilience, and recovery: Perspectives from the Kauai Longitudinal Study. *Development and Psychopathology*, *5*, 503–515.

Whitebook, M., & Bellm, D. (1999). *Taking on turnover*. Washington, DC: National Center for the Child Care Workforce.

Whitebook, M., Howes, C., & Phillips, D. (1990). *Who cares? Child care teachers and the quality of care in America*. Washington, DC: National Center for the Child Care Workforce.

Wyman, P. A., Cowan, E. L., Work, W. C., Hoyt-Meyers, L., Magnus, K. B., & Fagan, D. B. (1999). Caregivers and developmental factors differentiating young at-risk urban children showing resilient versus stress-affect outcomes. *Child Development*, *70*, 1456–1473.

Index

About the Authors

Carollee Howes, Ph.D., is a nationally and internationally recognized developmental psychologist focusing on children's social and emotional development. In 1981 she joined the faculty in the UCLA Department of Education, where she teaches in the Applied Developmental Ph.D. Program. She is on the Leadership Team of the National Center for Early Development and Learning. She has been conducting local and national research on children's experiences in child care and school including being principal investigator on the National Child Care Staffing Study, the Family and Relative Care Study, the Cost Quality and Outcomes Study, and the Early Head Start National Evaluation Study. Her research focuses on children's experiences in child care, their concurrent and long-term outcomes from child-care experiences, child-care quality, and efforts to improve child-care quality.

Sharon Ritchie has been in the field of education for 25 years. She earned her master's in special education from the University of Southern California in 1981, and her doctorate in education from UCLA in 1995. Throughout her career she has worked with emotionally disturbed children and their families as a teacher, a program director, an advocate and a researcher. She worked for 12 years as a teacher educator at UCLA's Center X, working with teachers to develop practices that carefully considered the cultural and economic contexts of their students' lives, and emphasized the need for developing warm and trusting relationships. She is engaged in ongoing studies of quality and practice in early childhood classrooms throughout the nation. Her research focuses on the importance of teachers in providing children a safe, secure environment in which they can learn and thrive.